MOVING IN THE

LIGHT

The Deb Bennett Story

by Von Braschler

author of

Seven Secrets of Time Travel

and

Confessions of a Reluctant Ghost Hunter

MOVING IN THE LIGHT

The Deb Bennett Story

Braschler, Von, 1947–

Moving in the Light, The Deb Bennett Story / Von Braschler

Paperback ISBN 978-0-9973754-6-6
Library of Congress Control Number: 2018938698

Published in the United States of America
by Shanti Publishing

SHANTI PUBLISHING

Dedicated to Gigi

Foreword
by Mari Coryell

Many years ago, I was considering applying for an administrative assistant position at Mount Hood Hospice. At the time I was the sole provider for my young son and accepting a position with a non-profit would be a substantial pay cut and yet the uniqueness of the opportunity was irresistible.

Little did I know that one of the enduring gifts that would come from working for Mount Hood Hospice would be a connection with someone whose friendship I have valued for over thirty years.

One of my new duties was to attend weekly business meetings where I met Von Braschler. I immediately felt an instant connection and comfort that seemed mutual.

As our friendship grew, Von and I explored many facets of spirituality together. We spent untold hours in a dark room experimenting with a homemade Kirlian camera. There were meditation circles and therapeutic touch sessions with friends, always exploring paths to connect and deepen our understanding of spirit.

Even though Von and I have lived hundreds of miles apart, our heart and spirit bond has never weakened. This bond is made of light and love and connection that goes beyond our current physical bodies.

We mutually recognized our spirit bond and reconnection when we met, and I believe we would again know it in whatever form we take next.

Von is proof in my life that some connections transcend time and space. And it is an amazing gift when I listen as the quiet voice speaks... "Here is someone special. Here is someone you have known before."

I was born into a Conservative Baptist, hell and brimstone, all American melting pot, 1950's family. This culture did not welcome exploratory questions from children about living and dying. I was too young to understand the impetus of my questions was an effort to learn the difference between religion and spirituality, but I did know that the Conservative Baptist rhetorical answers of "the will of God" really meant "shut up and go away." This created a personal culture bereft of any traditions beyond prayer to offer simple guidance when bearing witness to the process of dying.

In the early days of hospice, the cultural taboos surrounding death and dying were still deeply ingrained, and staff routinely fought the medical establishment to provide adequate pain control for patients. The standard answer was that the patient would become addicted to the drugs used to control pain. I always believed there were worse things than dying...like not being able to do the work necessary to die in comfort and dignity.

The hospice revolution created a support system built on normalization and loving acceptance of the process of shedding our physical body. In my experience hospice pushed the medical community into acceptance of their role to offer multi-modality measures of comfort to help ease a patient's final journey. And they taught the living how to gently bear witness and lovingly support the dying.

Unfortunately, in our culture, many of us still struggle with our own inadequacies when we learn a friend is dying. We have no history of tradition to lean on, no guides to offer us a path that is deeply ingrained in our collective psyche. What does supporting the process of dying even look or feel like? How can we participate in the healing of dying?

With this book, Von has distilled the final journey into its most simplistic essence. Be the Light. These three powerfully simple words are a guide to the living and the dying. Be the Light.

Three words we can put into practice; words that are a tool to create a healing space to experience vulnerability, acceptance, pain, love and suffering. A tool for letting go and becoming a supportive and loving witness to our shared journey. A final gift of loving support... Be the Light.

Mari Coryell

Co-author, *A Magical Journal: A Personal Journey through the Seasons of the Year*

Introduction

This is a true story about life transition. It is a journey that all of us will need to negotiate at some point. The problem for many people, however, is that they come to this crossroad with little foresight, confidence, or direction. Many people fear death as the end, even though it merely marks the end of physical viability. That's sort of like stubbornly sitting in an old automobile after the motor has died and the transmission has worn down. Our essential life force, soul, or spirit remains eternal. Our consciousness lives outside the body, as proven by countless accounts of near-death experiences, vision quests, out-of-body meditations, and even our dreams when spirit wanders beyond the body. We are light beings encased temporarily in a physical cocoon.

While most everyone has experienced profound and vivid dreams, many people approach death with fear and reluctance to move on. Their outer cocoon is the only tangible form that they recognize and trust, even when it begins to decay. Sadly, then, some people cling to their physical lives. Fear and confusion hold them fast in a dead-end place and time, stuck between the physical world and the world of spirit.

Hospice is a wonderful way for people who are terminally ill to plan this life transition. As light beings, everyone should be able to negotiate a personal escape outside the body into the world of light where spirit moves freely. To many, this opportunity for transformation might seem like a dark and overwhelming maze.

This book is about a young woman with terminal cancer who practiced walking through the maze and into the light with simple exercises done in the comfort of her bed. Readers familiar with *The Tibetan Book of the Dead* could recognize the approach as a way to practice dying and preparing for the transition.

Deb Bennett, the cancer victim in this story, was in her twenties when she first was diagnosed with a massive brain tumor. She lost all her hair, her son and husband through divorce, and much of her youth. Then she made a remarkable recovery and went into many years of remission. She was featured in a book about amazing cancer survivors and even spoke on the radio with the book's author.

I met Deb when she was thirty-two years old and ready to resume her life. She responded to an advertisement that I ran for rental space. I rented rooms in my large Victorian house to roommates who shared the house with me. She loved living there with her cats.

One of the things that I shared with Deb was information I had been given years earlier by a mysterious Indian mystic. He believed that we should be living in the light and moving in the light to truly awaken our spirit.

When Deb's cancer returned, the instruction from the yoga master from India proved to be priceless. We developed some meditation exercises to use the information as a guide to channel the light and move freely in the light, beyond time and space and even beyond death.

The irony, of course, is that we are all going to die, yet nobody really dies. Physical death is simply walking through one doorway and opening another door. The door we open can be filled with light and welcoming. Practicing this walk through the doorway is key to a seamless transition.

These actual events in the life of one remarkable cancer patient happened many years ago. I have chosen to write the story as a first-person narrative. although the story is about Deb and not about me. I was simply lucky enough to watch Deb's brave and glorious transformation beyond life and death.

Some of the names and events have been changed slightly, while other names and events have left my memory over the years. I have tried to tell Deb's story as straightforward as possible. I apologize in advance if anyone described in any part of the story finds the way I have told this story upsetting. It was not my intent to cast any blame, but simply to report. Deb blamed nobody for her early death. Why should anyone else?

Von Braschler
December, 2016

Table of Contents

Chapter 1
Spring 1988

A few years before I met Deb Bennett - the cancer survivor this book is about - I had a strange encounter with a man from India. His cryptic remarks prepared me for my journey through life and death with Deb in the years that followed.

This mysterious gentleman kept calling me on the telephone, but his calls made little sense to me at first. My impression was that he was calling me long-distance from India. At least, I initially believed that his calls originated in India. He sounded a million miles away; and the quality of the transmissions was pretty poor. He called me repeatedly to encourage me to move on, spiritually. He said that I needed to get on with my life and find my way. He also encouraged me to "live in the light." He professed, in fact, that personally living in the light had proven to be a magical formula for spiritual evolution.

His profound, yet simple insights into living in the light later guided my life and that of my future roommate Deb when things began to grow dark for her.

I still get a shiver up my spine whenever I recall the bizarre phone calls I received that summer from the stranger with the thick Indian accent. His soft voice made him sound very old and very wise. He called me several times at work with a personal invitation. Since I had never met this man before, I really had no idea who he was. And because he had such a thick East Indian accent and spoke softly, I wasn't certain exactly what he wanted from me at first.

At that time in my life, I was working at Quest Books in the Theosophical Society national headquarters at Wheaton, Illinois. I lived on the second floor of the publication building, with our own bookstore and shipping area on the floor below. Down the hall from where I lived, I shared a corner suite of offices with our production manager Mike King. My space was located in the far corner of the building with big windows that faced south. The corner office was overrun with house plants that seemed to love the bright, southern exposure. It was hot working in the light, but also exhilarating; and I often tiptoed down the hallway at night in my bathrobe to spend a few extra hours working in the corner office with all of the windows and plants.

Because my predecessor at Quest Books, Clarence "Pete" Petersen, had helped to start the book line and been publication director there so long, many people called my office phone expecting to find Pete. I mean, we had the same extension on the same phone number. Also, we worked in the same office with the same duties where he had worked so many years before retiring from publishing. So I got many curious calls in that office. None were stranger, though, than the one from the old Indian gentleman with an invitation for me to join him.

"Sir," he said initially, "I wish to invite you on a lightning tour of India in August. It will be a great experience for you. I can assure you of that. I lead a group every year at that time. The weather is good at that time of year. This is something that you really must do. Won't you join me?"

He told me his name and I tried to write it down as best I could understand him. It was a traditional East Indian name and hard for me to grasp. Still, when he called again to make the same personal plea, I became suspicious that the call might be some sort of hoax.

I began to question the legitimacy of the caller and his offer and probed other staff members to determine whether I'd been "pranked". I suspected my co-workers at the publication building and administration building across the street. There were limited possibilities. Most of the staff were women. Of the men who worked there, none were elderly or Indian. There was the editor of the magazine, our national secretary, a man who made videos, the gardener, the head of building maintenance, a librarian, the printer, and the guy who ran the audio department. Most of the voices were totally different pitches. It would be difficult for any of these men to stretch their natural voices to sound like the mystery man on the phone. And none of them, really, ever struck me as a practical joker or theatrical enough to pull off such a deception. That Indian accent sounded perfect.

I did question a couple of them, nonetheless. Nobody smiled, smirked, or twitched in any way that people often do when trying to trick someone. They just gave me odd looks and shook their heads, as though I was out of my mind. So, I asked the woman at the information desk that sometimes routed calls. My impression from speaking to the woman who ran that office was that all of my mysterious calls had come through directly by somebody who dialed my extension number without any internal assistance.

I was beginning to believe that these mysterious calls just might be genuine. And so, it continued. The kindly, old gentleman from India on those scratchy phone calls kept asking me to join him in late August for his annual "lightning tours of India."

The Theosophical Society has its international headquarters in southern India and people of India have long played a key role in our organization. But this man on the phone did not refer to the Theosophical Society or the international headquarters. He was referring to his own guided tours of India in late August; a time that he explained was best for travel there, due to the climate change at that time of year.

Eventually, I came to realize that this man was calling to me from somewhere more remote and distant than India. As it turned out, he was calling me from the great beyond. It took some time for me to reach this conclusion, however, because he sounded like a regular person – a sincere gentleman from India, who was soliciting my participation on a group tour that he was guiding. He was so kind and persuasive that it was hard to tell him no. But because I had no strong interest in such a trip and had only recently started my job at Quest Books, such a big excursion at that time was pretty much impossible for me.

I was totally engrossed in my new job. I had just helped to start *The Quest,* a new magazine. Also, I had started a syndicated radio show that went out to thirty-seven stations weekly called *The Eternal Quest.* Then, too, I was helping to organize new author videos for a self-syndicated television series in thirteen US markets. So, my days and nights were busy with new activities seven days a week while working at Quest Books for the Theosophical Society. Juggling all of these new projects, there was simply no time for me to disappear for a side trip across the world for a month or so. Also, such a guided trip to India would certainly be costly for somebody who worked at a non-profit organization, as I did. I tried to explain all of that to the gentleman with the thick Indian accent.

Still he called me a third time to ask once more. When I told him no again, he accepted that as my final decision, but asked me to keep such a trip in mind. He told me that such a trip to India would most certainly change my life and open my eyes.

He then gave me some advice on light, life, and reaching higher levels of consciousness. With his background as an Indian spiritual guide, I figured his free advice had to be significant. It seemed likely that such an Indian gentleman who led spiritual tours through Mother India was probably well trained in yoga and skilled in Eastern spiritual science with much to offer.

His advice to me was simple, however. First, he asked whether I meditated. I told him yes. And he asked how and when I did it.

I started to reconstruct in my mind the last times when I had meditated. I told him that I meditated wherever I found myself and at whatever time of day was convenient for me during the busy day. (I had been proud that I could reach a meditative state of sorts almost anywhere and anytime, even washing the dishes.)

There are different approaches to meditation, of course, as well as different types. Some people stare at a dot on the wall, gaze into a spinning paper twirler, or are hypnotically moved into a different mental space by the sound of a bell. There are different levels and expectations of meditation. I'm not certain exactly where I was in my spiritual growth back then, but I knew that I could reach some meditative state without prompts and reliably return to that state rather quickly and easily. I frankly don't think I was reaching a very deep and meaningful level of meditation at that point in my life, however. I don't believe I knew that higher levels were available to me.

The mystic on the phone suggested that I would reach higher states of consciousness and gain higher insights if I put more structure and planning into meditation, carefully selecting when and where I would do so. That way, I would not be distracted by sharing time with other activities that were not ideally suited for reaching higher states of consciousness.

To him, this was a fine art and could not be compromised. It embarrassed me to recognize that I had been doing what so many Americans do these days – attempting to multi-task. It was a little like driving a car while distracted. Meditation, if done correctly, needs our full attention.

"Are you near any water?" he asked me.

I described the pond in back of the Theosophical Society grounds and the lake at the park across the street.

"Are you able to get up early in the morning to meditate?" he asked me.

I indicated that I was. Sometimes, in fact, I would meditate with a group in a mediation room in the administration building across the street in the morning.

"You should try to meditate in the early morning light and beside water" he told me. "Running water is best," he added.

He suggested that the first light of the day each morning was ideal, and that running water was always better than stagnant water.

"Find the perfect light," he said. "There you will find harmony."

By the way he described it, I began to visualize a form of deeper meditation that was more than merely quiet reflection, but something quite moving. I visualized moving in the light. For the first time, I could really see that meditation was meant to be active and moving.

After that third call, I walked downstairs to our bookstore to check out the books by Indian authors, thinking he might be listed somewhere in an index. The Quest Book Shop sold many books from many publishers in addition to our own. In the book shop, I started pulling books on meditation off the shelf. To my surprise, I found that my mystery man was the author of books on meditation. He had a special technique for teaching meditation, whereby he encouraged students to seek the morning light and meditate there beside moving water. On the back of one book cover, his biographical description also noted that he was famous for organizing lightning tours of India in the early fall. This biographical description listed his date of birth and the date of his death.

So, I had been speaking to a ghost, a spirit who knew something profound about moving in the light. I had heard of strange calls from beyond and knew that there was a recognized body of case studies in this area of spirit communications. Ghosts were known on occasion to reach out by electronic forms of communication readily available to us, speaking through our radios, televisions, and telephones. I actually knew people who had received such strange phone calls, so didn't doubt that it was possible and legitimate.

But why did he call me? Did he think that I was Pete, my predecessor? Or maybe he just asked for the person who occupied my position there. Not once, however, did he refer to any other person or the organization for which I worked.

Naturally I visited the pond in the back of the Theosophical national headquarters, a stagnant pool that held some lazy carp. It was shrouded by beautiful, old trees that bent down to the ground near the fence line of the 40-acre property that we called "the campus."

I never discussed this with other staff members at Quest Books or the Theosophical Society because I had already pestered many of them with questions about my mysterious phone calls.

They knew nothing about the calls, they were meant only for me. Or at least that's what I thought at the time.

I figured that the mystic's personal calls to me should stir me to make some changes in my life and how I viewed the world and our place in it. Here was a man who called me from beyond the veil of what we normally consider the dividing point between life and death, yet he found death to be no barrier. Just how energizing was light, I wondered, and just how could living in the light move me spiritually to new heights? After all, I had seen and experienced light all of my life. Light was all around us. It was warm and bright. Could it have other properties that seem less obvious? Could the light actually transform me?

Eventually, I reasoned that this old man would not bother to call me repeatedly from the spirit realm to simply wax poetic, but really wanted to ignite me to open my eyes to something not obvious – namely the metaphysical, innate power in light as energy.

Studying crystals and magnetic stones, I began to see that energy around us can be naturally absorbed, transformed, and transmitted. Light as electromagnetic radiation releases down upon us to be absorbed and processed, making us dynamos for processing energy. But could we do that more efficiently and with better results?

Certainly, meditation in early morning light beside water seemed like a more intensive way to enter a state of heightened awareness. It occurred to me, probably for the first time, that the proper environment could energize my personal voyages into consciousness development.

So, I started to change the way I mediated. I got up earlier and meditated outdoors in the morning light. While I didn't have a brook, river, or ocean near me, I did have a beautiful pond near my home. While I didn't have running water beside me – the ideal location which the Indian mystic had recommended, I nonetheless had a pond where the morning light danced upon the surface with a shimmering glitter.

I brought a blanket and lay it on the moist grass in the early morning light, with the evening dew still heavy on the ground. It was quiet there and an ideal place to meditate. I noticed that the quality of the natural light is different early in the day, with a softness, gentleness, and feeling of great potential. By meditating there early in the day far from the main road at the far end of the property, it was easy to find a quiet and stillness that is ideal for meditation. My meditations there were not simply quiet moments of inner reflection and concentration, but the opportunity for great release. Beside the water with steam rising off the surface in the gentle morning light, I could access a still point deep within me, focus my intent, and release my consciousness to soar far beyond my body. I found the light to be liberating; and I could ride it like waves of boundless energy. And I did reach higher levels of consciousness when I meditated in the light.

I also came to realize that we received a different quality of light each morning. Some days the light was softer, while other days it was more intense. I even began to notice a difference in the color of light from day to day. Before, I had always thought of natural light as white; but there are subtle color variations from day to day. I studied both the science of light and the metaphysical properties of light. I even studied mystical discussions on the magical properties of light of varying color and the possibilities that each color of light held for us. It was quite an awakening.

Since Illinois winters are much colder than winters in India, I would forgo my morning meditations by the outside pond on many inclement days. I began to miss the experience on those days indoors, because the natural light outdoors had changed me. I could feel the difference.

I started to wonder about traveling in the light, since my meditations were taking me to new levels outside my body, where time and space did not seem to exist. My studies included Hindu Samadhi mystics who taught their initiates to meditate deeply, leaving the physical world behind and experiencing life outside normal time and space. Apparently Native American shamans and dream walkers experienced life outside time and space when they went into deep shamanic trances and explored the past and future to bring back insight to their people. When I realized that Albert Einstein was a mystic who had studied the mystical classic *The Secret Doctrine*, suddenly his writings about time measured by light as it strikes us became deeply insightful and meaningful for me.

This led me to study, write, and speak on the subject of light, color, consciousness development, and time. I could see that time was no barrier for consciousness that could live and move in light.

I recall walking into an esoteric bookstore in Chicago in those years of discovery and being drawn toward one corner of the room where a dark, greenish stone of great weight and magnetic quality called to me. I lifted it gently into two cupped hands and carried it directly to the checkout counter. When I was asked whether I knew what the stone was, I told the clerk about electromagnetism and magnetic stones. I spoke about lodestones and magnetite and the philosopher's stone. The clerk told me that the Magnetite stone had apparently spoken to me; and that it was mine without charge.

With the help of a gifted friend, I began operating a Kirlian camera that her handy brother had built. It seemed to measure energy discharge in the body after electrical stimulation – very different from normal cameras that measure light reflected off objects.

Also, about the same time, I became fascinated with energy healing and using the energy within us and all around us to transfer electromagnetic energy to other living bodies to stimulate their self-regenerative process.

I began to notice that my energy responded differently to the natural light energy available at different times of the day. The morning light would be softer and filled with excellent energy for beginning new projects and undertaking new activities.

Yes, this mysterious, old man with the East Indian accent seemed to know something about the nature of things. He seemed to know a lot about energy and potential. And he wanted to motivate me. He was directing me toward the light.

I moved away from Illinois and my work at the Theosophical Society headquarters. I worked for Stillpoint's owner and publisher Lady Meredith Young-Sowers, who also is author of the bestselling book *Agartha* and other books. While there, I worked on various books like Dan Millman's first book and John Robbin's book *Diet for a New America*. Then I accepted a job in publishing in the Twin Cities when I left Stillpoint in New Hampshire to take a job in Saint Paul at Llewellyn Publications.

In time I was leading workshops in Kirlian photography where electrically charged material experienced radiation discharge and seemed to send energy outward from the physical body after electrical stimulation. It was amazing to me how the Kirlians, a husband and wife research team in Russia, simultaneously conducted near-death experiments to determine measurable changes in the human body when death would appear imminent.

More significantly, perhaps, I started writing drafts and outlines for future books on energy, time, and consciousness development. It began to occur to me that there was a much bigger message to the mystic's advice to live in the light, a message that was not for me alone. I began to think about not only living in the light, but moving in the light. Where could the light take us? My meditations beside the pond had showed me that it could take me literally out of my body, as my consciousness separated from the confines of my physical core to a place where normal time and space did not seem to exist.

I hunkered down in a hundred-year-old Victorian house in St. Paul with my cat and decided to share the oversized three-story building with roommates who could help me pay down the large mortgage and maybe watch my cats when I was away. From time to time I needed to travel for Llewellyn and really needed someone close to feed the cat and water my Aloe Vera plants. At least, that's what I told myself.

Spirit was beginning to direct my life in this new way, as the old mystic on the phone had suggested might happen. I guess I didn't really need to take his "lightning tour" of India to discover who I was. In a way, his mysterious phone calls had changed my life forever. I just needed to meditate in the light.

Chapter 2
March 1992

When I interviewed for the job in St. Paul with Llewellyn, I flew into the city on one borrowed day from my employer to meet the staff and possibly scout the area for housing. I had not been able to find an affordable house to buy previously and was encouraged to find many affordable Victorian homes on the market in St. Paul. That was late February of 1991. I blew into town, was treated by my prospective employer to a day in a local hotel and had just enough time after interviews at Llewellyn to check out one big, Victorian home near my intended employer. I was not promised the job at the time I viewed the Victorian home but thought it best to arrange for immediate housing anyway, just in case I needed to move there fast.

I remember riding in a taxi with just an address clipped from the newspaper. The driver eventually found the house. It was a three-story, blue house complete with turret, second-floor balcony, and wrap-around front porch. It was old, build in 1895 and needed fresh paint.

The woman who rented me a room there was surprised that I took the room on the spot. It was a third-story bedroom next to a full bath. The space was a remodeled attic with a funky, slanted roof. She had me sign a six-month lease and leave her with a deposit. Then I went back home and waited to see whether my phone would ring with good news about the job. I honestly believe that my disclosure of signing a lease on blind faith of a forthcoming job offer ultimately convinced the publisher that he should offer me the job. His initial tone on the phone sound conciliatory. His tone changed a little when I told him that I had already rented a place to live there in anticipation of working for him. One month later, I loaded a U-Haul trailer and headed to St. Paul to live in the Victorian house.

Only a few months after I had moved into the house, the owner declared that she wanted to sell the house and move to Texas. Consequently, I was fortunate to buy the house only ten months after coming there as a renter. When I purchased the house and moved into the large, master bedroom, my original bedroom quickly became a potential room for me to rent.

I figured my three-story historic house in the old part of town was going to be too big for me, my cat Zeke, and the giant Aloe Vera plants that had accompanied us to Minnesota. I ran an ad for a roommate almost immediately to find someone nice who liked cats and houseplants enough to watch things for me, since I would be traveling to book fairs and book distributors on behalf of my new employer Llewellyn Publications.

I think my advertisement for the space in the local newspaper read something like, "Share our

Victorian home in Saint Paul. Big kitchen. Two baths. I'll shovel the snow, but you must like cats."

One of the first persons to answer my ad for a roommate was Deb Bennett, a young woman who had looked death in the face and bounced back smiling. Deb had this big smile of someone who felt happy just to be alive; and her whole face radiated a sort of glow.

She was a young thirty-two years old. Deb was tall and thin and had one of the brightest, ready smiles that you've ever seen. Her face glowed red when she smiled, as though she contained light inside her that spilled over with genuine cordiality and enthusiasm. Her hair was fine and golden like the sun in summer, and she pulled it back into a tight ponytail. Her round head sported beauty marks and sharp, chiseled facial features that jumped right out at you. Still, she had a reserved quietness about her, as though she held something inside.

But when I first met Deb Bennett in early March of 1992, it never occurred to me that she could be dead of natural causes within one year. When she responded to my ad for new roommate, she beamed with enthusiasm. When I spoke with her at length about moving into the old Victorian house in Saint Paul, she was radiant with vitality, the very picture of health.

I poured her a cup of tea; and we sat at the kitchen table. I found chatting with her very easy, as though we were siblings or very old friends.

She told me that she was a good renter, no matter what her current landlord might say about her. I told her that I wasn't so much looking for a renter as a good roommate who loved cats.

She jumped all over that comment with the admission that she had two cats herself. I had recently taken in a stray as a companion to my gray Maine Coon cat from Illinois, so we had a lot in common already.

We talked for some time about nothing but cats, the way two cat lovers will do when put together to swap stories. Apparently, her cats meant a lot to her and had been a vital part of her life.

Then she started to tell me about an illness that had nearly taken her life. She'd had inoperable brain cancer and gone through chemotherapy. It looked grim.

Along the way, she lost her husband and the custody of her only child - a son named Jamie.

She was alone and dying. And the cancer engulfed her and sidelined her for many years. Deb told me that she didn't feel much support, either, as she grew weaker and weaker. She lost her hair and most of her strength.

Deb shared the following story with me: One day when she was out with her mother hanging clothes on a line, apparently her mother commented that it was embarrassing to have her daughter appear outdoors without any hair and that she should wear a wig.

She put down her tea cup to look at me directly.

"The building where I've been living is unsafe," she said. "I have been living there with another woman sharing an apartment. But now we need to move and soon. We did a little yard work. We offered to do work on the building, too, because it needs serious attention. My landlord there might not give me good references to move, but there's two sides to that story. The building's a mess. I can see that, but they can't.

"Anyway, your ad caught my attention. Sharing a house, getting a room in a big house like this is something I could probably afford. And where I've been living is a mess, so I want out now. There's got to be an easier way to live. I just need a quiet, clean place for me and my cats."

I told her that the rent for her bedroom and sharing the rest of the house with complete kitchen and laundry privileges would be $295 month, plus an equal share of the household utilities. I told her what those utilities included and usual cost. It would have added seventy-five extra dollars per month on average. She said that she worked at Dayton Hudson Department store at a big mall in nearby Roseville, where she ran the cosmetic counter. She wasn't drawing manager's pay, however. They paid her a little more than $6 per hour. She said she liked the place and hoped to hear from me soon, after I had processed her rental application and checked her references.

I called the next day to offer her the rental, but she said that it was unlikely she could afford it, after adding in the utility costs. That seemed like a shame to me; as she had to move and was losing her roommate from the condemned building.

About an hour later, I called her back to say she could pay just $295 a month and to forget about the utility charges. It would be nice, I figured, to have a cat-friendly person at the house to look after my felines when I might be gone. Deb thanked me and said she could move in immediately.

She brought her cats over to meet my cats. Her cats were named Wizard and Willow. They had been with her for some time.

"Wizard saved my life," she told me.

I was waiting for some dramatic story of a fire with the cat screaming at her to get outside.

"Wizard helped me during those years when I was sick," Deb explained. Looking at Deb now, however, I thought that she couldn't be more than thirty years old. So I asked how long she'd been sick.

"I was sick for many years and not expected to live," she said. "I had cancer and went through treatment with no major results. I kept getting worse. I lost all of my hair. I couldn't do much of anything. And people had pretty much given up on me. But not Wizard. He sat by me, day and night, purring and sending me love. I can thank him for bringing me back. Everyone else had pretty much written me off."

Looking at her rental application, as she spoke, I saw that she had lost custody of her son during this long illness. She was now alone, except for the cats.

"A lady wrote a book about amazing cancer stories - about recovery and put me in her book. When she went on the radio to talk about her book, she'd have me on the radio, too."

I asked whether her parents lived in the area and whether she had any brothers or sisters. Her parents lived in the next town over and had one younger daughter. Deb said they'd pretty much give her up for dead and that her mother told her that Deb's loss of hair embarrassed her. She urged her to wear a wig rather than show the world her true condition.

Despite the setback, Deb did recover and now went into a clinic every few months for cat scans to determine whether the cancer in her brain had returned. She got a job a Dayton Hudson Department Store in the cosmetic counter and spent the day showing women customers how to look their best.

During Deb's years of decline, she had lost her husband and custody of her only son, although she maintained contact with him. Deb's dad helped her get a little red car to commute to work at her $6.85-hour job running a cosmetics counter in a department store without the title of manager that might have gone with it. She had a red blazer given to her by one cosmetics line to represent the company. Whenever women walked through their store, Deb would try to entice them to stop by for a makeover.

Deb desperately needed a new place to live, after the confrontation with the landlord over building concerns. She reiterated how she and her roommate had brought their concerns about building safety problems to the owner, who apparently made no immediate changes. Deb said they were especially disappointed in his reaction, because they'd helped maintain the yard and only wanted to alert the owner to what needed fixing. When they failed to get his cooperation, Deb contacted the city building inspections department to discuss her concerns. They apparently advised her to withhold rent until the problems with the building were corrected to her satisfaction. The city also inspected the building and "red tagged" the rental units, meaning they couldn't be rented until necessary corrections to the building were made. At least, that's what Deb told me; and I found her to be transparent and sincere.

"We told the guy who owns our building that there were problems that really need to be fixed," she explained between slurps of black coffee. "It was getting dangerous to stay there, because of the condition of the building." She put down her coffee cup to look directly at me.

"I'm really not a problem renter," she said. "It's just that this other building was unsafe, we felt. But the man who owned the building, our landlord, didn't live there. He just couldn't see it or didn't want to see it.

"Well, we tried to work with him. We did a little yard work. We offered to do work on the building, but it needed serious attention. So, we finally reported the problems with the building to the city. They advised us to withhold rent, until the repairs were made.

"Personally, I didn't even want to wait that long. But we did. We will probably lose our deposit. And it could be very expensive to move out on my own, without my roommate, to find a new place.

I asked her whether the landlord was working with the city on building corrections, or whether she was just bailing on him now.

"The city came by the building and just tagged everything that was defective. They gave him only so long to fix things; but he doesn't seem ready to make the changes. The landlord turned around and threatened to evict us."

Her friends seemed to be mostly people at work. She worked pretty hard and liked her job. And she had her two cats.

Deb smiled softly with a crooked, little smile and said she just felt lucky to be alive and healthy again.

In March of 1992, she moved into my house with Wizard and Willow. Deb radiated life like a person reborn and given new energy. Soon she had moved her favorite wicker rocking chair in front of the living room television where she could get a more comfortable view of the TV. She loved to watch Star Trek and tried not to miss any of the original series reruns whenever they were scheduled.

I remember Deb backing into the house with that big wicker rocker of hers and placing it squarely in from of the TV in the living room, about four feet from the screen. Then she dragged in box after box of things carefully wrapped, which she squirreled away in the linen closet next to her third-floor bedroom and next to the third-floor bathroom.

"These are things that keep me occupied," was all that she would say about the boxes she put in the linen closet. These mystery boxes didn't seem all that heavy, but were crammed with things known only to Deb, like little treasures she couldn't share or even talk about. I could see that she was a private person who lived a quiet life of reflection and inner peace.

Along with her wicker rocker, she dragged a matching wicker foot stool through the door and into the living room, to go in front of the rocker. And then she popped through the front door with the wicker piece that made the set complete – a wicker basket, that I figured would hold magazines and newspapers, but turned out to be a stuffed toy box of cat toys for Mr. Wizard and Willow.

Deb made several trips between the apartment building that she was fleeing and our old, Victorian house with its witch's hat turret and wrap-around country porch in front. She provided quite a colorful contrast when she carried armload after armload of bright red blazers to the porch of the tall, blue house. And she made the toil seem almost classy, as she sprang up the steps with her long, easy strides and her stylish hat bouncing on her blond head.

There seemed to be a lot of synchronicity in her life at the house and the things that she brought there with her. She worked at Dayton's department store; and she had both a microwave that said Dayton and also a clock that said Dayton. Even more intriguing was the way the house seemed to fit her. The old built-in wall heater in our kitchen where she placed her clock and microwave had long carried the Dayton imprint. Dayton had put its mark on Deb and now on me and the house we shared, as well. For better or worse, our lives were intertwined.

I totally stopped thinking about her as a victim, as a person who had a brain tumor that went into remission and appeared on the radio and in a book as a miraculous cancer survivor. But part of me wondered why I was so willing to cut her a deal to live at the house at a discount, to escape her current living condition. Clearly, she had to move on. My approach had been to avoid people with baggage or people who were moving away from something in their lives. I once broke a promising relationship with a woman that I worked with at a newspaper only because she confided in me that she had a brain tumor. People with brain tumors dropped dead eventually. But not Deb. She had beaten it. She had a new lease on life.

In time, Deb had made enough trips in her little, red Korean car to bring everything to outfit her bedroom, too. She carried an ironing board, television, stereo set, and furniture up to the third floor. I couldn't believe her enthusiasm and the lightness of her footwork, as she quietly zipped up and down the stairs, seemingly without growing tired. And she beamed with happiness.

After she had put everything she owned in its proper place in the new kitchen, living room, and her bedroom upstairs, she started to explore. As I puttered around the kitchen, I found her opening drawers and looking in corners with wide eyes. She told me how much she loved the old Victorian house.

Just before she'd moved into the house, the house was put onto the Saint Paul Tour of Homes as a good example of Victorian remodeling. The joke, I suppose, was that the old house was originally not a Victorian house at all. I remember seeing photos from the local historical society that showed tennis enthusiasts in their 1920's bloomers with wooden rackets playing on the site of an old pond the city had once called a little Ramsey Park. The tennis court covered over the muddy pond and overlooked a small bluff with a square, two-story house directly below it. That was the origins of my Victorian house. The foundation was apparently poured in 1890 and the house built in 1895. When the house was put on the market and simultaneously put on the Tour of Homes in the fall of 1991, it became apparent from some of the visitors who filled in the information gaps of the old house that it was redesigned to look more and more Victorian during the 1960s and 1970s. Apparently, somebody had been impressed by a visit to the President Warren G. Harding home in Marion, Ohio. Yes, the house was redesigned externally to look like the Harding home, with a turret, slate blue and cream exterior paint, wrap-around front porch, and a private balcony on the third floor.

During the tours, I sat in a corner of the living room as one of the renters who shared the house and had a room there. I soaked up as many of the stories about the old house that I could. The turret and third-floor addition had been slapped together by a man who called his remodeling company Fly by Night Construction Company. Apparently, our Victorian house was his only paying customer, although he did build his own house and had photos to prove it.

I learned that homeless people camped in the house and stripped out all of the copper and started a campfire in the kitchen during a time when it was between occupants. That lead to a complete kitchen rebuilding. The new kitchen was immense, which suited my landlady as a caterer just fine.

During that time, I lived in the corner bedroom on the third floor next to the bathroom and linen closet – the same room that Deb came to occupy in the early spring of 1992, a month or two after I bought the house, releasing my landlady to move to Texas.

Curiously, Texas was about the only place outside of Minnesota where Deb had ever lived. She told me that she hadn't been anywhere or done much of anything in her thirty-two years. She married young and had one child. Then she got sick for years and took many years to recover. In Texas, she struggled to survive as a low-paid cashier in a convenience store.

But all of that was behind her now, along with the landlord who was reportedly reluctant to bring her previous home up to safety code and then apparently tried to evict her after she reported him. Deb was now healthy, working, and happy. And she kept telling me how much she loved living in our Victorian house.

Every morning, she would put on one of those bright, red blazers and drive in her little, red car to work at the cosmetics counter in the Roseville Mall. She would come home dragging after a long day of meeting with people, giving passers-by a free facial makeover, setting up her little counter for new products and sale signs, and then figuring whether her department's sale total for the day measured up to expectations against projections and last-year sales figures.

But when she came through the door of our Victorian home, her slumping form would give way to an erect posture and a smile, happy to be home at last. And then she would watch Star Trek reruns in her wicker rocker and explore the many nooks and crannies of the old house.

Deb and I were pretty much alone in the big house that first year I owned it, as our other two housemates were rarely home. So, our house was quiet and roomy.

One day after returning home from Dayton's and spending a couple of quiet hours in her bedroom on her own, Deb stuck her head into my bedroom down the hall. My door was always open, so that my own cats could come and go at their leisure.

I was at the keyboard in the corner of my bedroom where the turret formed a small circular space with wrap-around windows. Admittedly, I was looking out the windows at the first spring leaves that were forming on the trees. But I was also pecking away at a word processor, writing a book about living and moving in the light, inspired in part by the spirit of the old Indian gentleman who called me on the phone back in Illinois.

Deb leaned into the room, with the bulk of her body twisted outside the door frame, so that only her head projected around the corner. She smiled awkwardly, as though caught snooping, but wanting to strike up a conversation.

"So, you actually work up here," she chirped, "- inside the turret room!"

"Caught me," I said, looking up from the keyboard of the old Brother Whisper Writer. "I'm working on a book, actually."

"Oh, what about?" she asked with genuine interest.

"I think I want to call it something like 'Moving in the Light,'" I said with a little hesitation.

"So, what's that all about?" Deb said.

"It will be about this mysterious, old man – a sage, who called me from India," I started to say. "Oh, well, I didn't actually meet him in person, but spoke with him on the phone several times. He was some sort of Hindu sage, who knew all about meditation in the light and living in the light. It got me really thinking about things on a deeper level."

"So, it's about light?" she asked. "I love metaphysical subjects – the deeper mysteries and truths."

"Are you into esoteric studies at all?" I asked her.

She shrugged. "I guess you could say that I was raised Catholic. Now, I'm looking deeper, I think. My favorite place to go is the woods in summer for We Fest. Wild girls."

"Well, I started to work on a book about the deeper mysteries of life, as experienced by animals who live a pure relationship of harmony with nature," I said. "Elephants mourn death like no other animals on earth. Whales form protection rings around sick or sleeping members of their pod. It was the birds who inspired us to fly, and the tiger who taught us speed and cunning. They are pure souls who live in perfect harmony with nature. And nature is spirit, don't you think?"

"So, you're writing about nature and animals?"

"In the light, yes. Living and moving in the light. See, I think living in the light is everything. It's the secret to becoming a master of time and space, evolving spiritually."

Deb blinked.

"Crazy, huh?" I asked.

"No, no," she said. "I was just thinking. I used to think that if I died when I had the cancer (and they said it was terminal) that the day would come when there would just be blackness – that I would continue, but that all that I could really see or experience was darkness."

"Do you still think that?" I asked her.

"I'm not so sure," she said. "I think there's some part of us that is eternal or immortal and goes on. So there is no darkness. Only light - right?"

"Well," I replied, "I'm starting to believe very strongly now that it's the physical limitations we experience in a dense, physical body that prevents us from stepping outside time and space and traveling as light beings. I mean, light is pure energy. As light beings encased in a physical body, we cannot ordinarily experience traveling as light at light speed. We are grounded, dragged down by our dense material form. If we could travel as pure light beings outside the body, then we could actually time travel and – as spirit, go anywhere, anytime in the blink of an eye, so to speak."

"But we are physical bodies," she said, "so we can't do that, right?"

"Or can we?" I posed.

"Hmm," Deb mused. "You like tea, right? I made some downstairs; and it's just about ready."

She opened the door a little wider, as though to draw me away from my corner of the room, hiding behind the keyboard. It was hot upstairs, as the heat rises quickly to the top floor in a three-story house. I was ready for a break and some conversation with the mystery lady who just moved in.

Downstairs in our large kitchen, I sat down in the kitchenette table area, while Deb went to the counter for the tea that she had brewed. She set out a couple of cups from the counter and began to pour.

"I have been thinking over the years, as I waited to die," she said, "just how limited our lives are, like a clock ticking down until it completely winds down and stops."

She turned her head suddenly to look out the kitchen window at the big trees on the boulevard.

"Now I realize that's not true," she said. "It just seems that way when you can see things that wind down – like a physical body wearing down. There seem to be just so many beats of the heart. Just so many hours. Our time seems limited."

"Don't you think that depends on your situation?" I asked, trying to bring her back.

"Yes, that's it," she said. "A new lease on life changes your perspective."

I sipped on my tea. There was a lemon under taste, a subtle distinction. I smiled my satisfaction.

She sat down across the table from me and circled her cup with a thoughtful hand.

"I used to think about being locked in place, in the hospital and later at home in bed," she mused, "never well enough to move about freely. I was a sick person with a fake wig and fixed expression with no time left. There was no light in my world."

"Fake wig?" I asked.

"Yeah, fake hair," she said. "I had to wear a wig. See, when you undergo chemotherapy, a little part of you dies every day. Your hair falls out. You don't look like a real person, just a shriveled-up thing. So people wear wigs. That doesn't really change anything for you, but it makes people feel better around you, like you're almost normal and nothing to stare at...."

"I'll bet you're glad that's all behind you," I offered.

"The wig doesn't always help. It didn't work with my mother. I have this lasting image of hanging clothes on the line with her one summer day, dressed in my wig." Deb shook her head and closed her eyes.

"I remember it like yesterday," she said. My mother said, 'Why do you wear that stupid thing? It's embarrassing.'"

"It embarrassed you or her?" I asked.

"Her. I only wore the wig for her. I seemed to embarrass her if my head was bald and if I wore a fake wig. Either way, it wasn't natural."

"Want to hear about the idea for my book?" I said, eager to change the subject, if only to take her mind off the old pain. In truth, I really didn't like talking about the book, especially at this early stage of its development.

Deb smiled and looked up at me, nodding her head.

"Well, it's about light and time," I said. "Everything that's truly alive and healthy and energized lives in the light. Light enlivens us all. Not just plants. We absorb light, process it, and project it. We are light beings wrapped in dense outer shells. The shell is all we really see; so most people think that's all we are. And they accept the limitations of the physical world.

"But light initializes us, lights us up. When light strikes you, depending on where you stand in the world, that determines how you experience *Now*. That's sorta what Einstein said.

"If we could move with the light at the speed of light, we could step outside the physical limitations of time and space. But that's hard to do in physical bodies. Matter that accelerates at the speed of light turns into pure energy.

"The only way I see that we can move in the light and transcend the physical limitations of time and space, then, is with our consciousness and invisible energy body. Our spirit can leave the body and travel, as pure energy through space and time without restrictions. And our spirit longs to be free."

I looked into Deb's eyes. She was processing some of it.

"I think Mr. Wizard, my cat, can do that," she finally said. "I think he leaves his body. He does more than sleep when he checks out all day long. He comes back with fire in his eyes. Know what I mean?"

"Yeah," I said. "And sometimes, on certain occasions, I think people like you and I leave our bodies in the same way. And we move with the light. That ever happen to you?"

I could see that I had stumped her, but that she was thinking, as though sorting out old mysteries that might have a new key to understanding.

"Well, when I was very sick, sometimes I would try to escape the pain and my body. I would travel someplace, just for a little while. But I would always come right back. So that's probably not the same thing, right? I mean, we all daydream."

"Ah, yes. Our dreams," I said. "In researching this book, I discovered that there are a lot of people who claim we actually do leave our bodies in our dreams and travel in our energy bodies. The Hindu Samadhi mystics train their students to leave their bodies and travel outside normal time and space by first learning to control their dreams."

"You know, I think I've had dreams like that," Deb slowly answered. "I thought it was wishful thinking, just dreaming of something I couldn't have, you know."

"And yet you have seen things and people clearly and vividly," I said. "You have detailed memories of places that were not part of your remembered past travels in the ordinary sense. You have out-of-this-world, vivid encounters on another plane of existence in another reality outside of your physical world."

Deb poured us both a little more tea, as though to encourage the conversation to continue.

"Think of people who have accidents and have the real experience of leaving their bodies," I suggested. "It happened to my son on a bicycle trip in Canada once. Just as a car behind him was about to run over him, I saw him rise up and then miraculously escape injury. Somehow the car ran over him without hurting him. But just before the car struck the bike, I saw my son rise up. I don't know any other way to explain it. And I don't think he does, either. But I think his higher self was involved. His spirit left his body and then saved him. I wish you had been there, so I could make you see what my eyes saw, but my mind cannot yet explain."

"Yes, people in emergency situations sometimes do miraculous things," Deb added.

"I was in a car accident myself once where my spirit left my body," I said. "Or at least that's the way it seemed. And I avoided a tragic accident because of it."

"Where?" she asked.

"Oh, I used to work at a newspaper in Anacortes, Washington, years ago. I had a little Triumph roadster and came barreling down a mountain hill. I was approaching a 90-degree turn to the left at the bottom of the hill, where a steel barricade blocked the steep bluff below. But I came roaring down the concrete road in my sports car, confident that I could turn left on a dime."

"What happened?" Deb asked.

"Well, I got to the bottom of the hill and saw a deep puddle of water on the road, where the rain from the night before had collected. How could I turn in that puddle of water? I would hydroplane and not make the hairpin turn, especially at that speed. But it was too late. I was already at the bottom of the hill when I saw the puddle of water."

I hesitated telling the rest of the story and closed my eyes.

"And then what happened?" she prompted.

"Well, I got really still and collected myself somewhere deep inside me. And then I could feel something rising up inside me. Time seemed to stand still. I seemed to freeze in place. Suddenly, I had all of the time in the world and could look calmly at various alternatives to work things out. It was all so strange.

"I thought about braking but realized that wouldn't work. Then I considered turning off the engine and discounted that. I even had time to think about turning the wheel hard left and taking my chances. I realized that I couldn't crash through the barricade. Either the steel barricade would destroy me on impact, or I would crash through it and go over the steep embankment."

"So, what happened?" Deb asked.

"I actually had time to work it all out. I played out the whole thing in my head. Then I did the unthinkable. I waited until the last instant when I was about to crash into the barricade and then downshifted all the way to first gear. I turned the steering wheel hard to the left, and then hit the gas, accelerating in first gear. The car was screaming to be traveling so fast in first gear."

"Did that work?"

"Uh, huh," I said, closing my eyes again. "It worked perfectly. The wheels spun madly to catch whatever pavement it could, and the car spun around like a top. I hit a glancing blow against the steel barricade but didn't get hurt or even damage the car much. It did leave a mark on that steel barricade, though."

"I'll bet you were relieved," Deb said.

"I was out of it for some time after that," I said. "I was out of my mind. I drove around town after I came all the way down the hill. I was still half out of my body. I was numb."

"Wow," she said.

"I have to think that my higher consciousness, my inner spirit, kicked in and took charge. It had no problem with time and space. It was operating literally at the speed of light."

We sat there for a few second and then sipped on our tea. After a while, Deb looked deeply at me.

"I used to think about time being fixed, like fate," she said, "as though life's beginning and end were running out of our control like some sort of destiny that we couldn't control. Maybe that was my cancer talking. When you're dying of cancer, you think about abrupt endings and a personal lack of control."

"But you beat the cancer," I reminded her. "You had a lot of control over your life, didn't you?"

"Sometimes, I think it was my cat Wizard that brought me through it," Deb said. "He would sit by me and rub against me. I know he understood that I was sick. He wouldn't leave my side. He would knead his little paws in me - not with sharp claws, but like a kitten. And he would heat up when he did that. He was warm to the touch, like he was on fire with energy. I would pet him, and sometimes I would get a shock off him when I rubbed him."

"Life is very precious," I said. "We all deserve to be well and happy. We don't live our lives to suffer. People who sit out in the sunlight and fresh air seem to be happier. It's even considered therapeutic. So, I see this whole thing about time and consciousness as a part of our search for health and well-being. It's really about being whole and complete, isn't it?"

"I guess," she said. "Being healthy and feeling whole again is something new to me. I think I took it for granted when I was little, but maybe I was already on my way to becoming sick even then."

"I mentioned an Indian gentleman upstairs," I told her. "I didn't mean like a shaman or Indian chief. He had a thick accept like someone from India who had learned his formal English from the British. Anyway, he kept calling me on the phone to talk about meditating in the early morning sunlight beside water – moving water, if possible. He saw it as a way to release the higher self, our inner spirit. He kept talking about the natural light, as though it was transformative."

"So, did you ever get together with him and learn to meditate like that?" Deb asked.

"I never met him face to face, but I did follow his advice. I began to meditate beside a pond in the morning light," I said. "It was a pond on the grounds where I worked and lived in Illinois. It was special. I could feel the light work on me, as though awaking my soul. And those meditations were very different. I did have lucid dreams, as though I was leaving my body during the meditations. I could go anywhere. And time stood still."

"So, it works," Deb said.

"Oh, yes," I said. "He really knew what he was talking about. But I never met the man personally. He just kept calling me on the phone."

"Sounds kind of mysterious," Deb said.

"Yeah," I said. "Mysterious. A mystery man. It turned out that he was dead, a spirit. I guess spirit communication isn't all that unique. It's happened to others. But it had never happened to me before then. He kept calling me at work and encouraging me to join him on a lighting tour of India. He promised that it would change my life. Then he would tell me how to meditate in the light. Even now, I find it hard to believe that he called me. And not just once, but again and again. Live in the light. That's what he seemed to want to tell me. Live and move in the light."

"So, he was a real ghost?" Deb asked.

"Well, yes," I said. "I guess so. Only he actually called me on the phone – several times in fact, and we had prolonged conversations. It wasn't just him speaking to me. I mean, we had a real exchange, a conversation. I think that's unusual. Spirit conversations aren't usually that elaborate. This man seemed highly engaged in what we might call the real world, the physical world."

"But how can you be sure he was dead?"

"Good question. How can anyone be sure when they are dead? What is death, really? I don't think we just close our eyes and fade to black. I think the eternal spirit that exists inside every one of us continues forever. It's a divine spark – electromagnetic energy. We are light beings. Once the physical wrapping is gone, the light being is free. We become a free spirit. We have this limited idea about life and death all wrong. That gentleman from India knew that. He knew all about living and moving in the light."

"But he sounded normal on the phone - like anyone would sound on the phone?" Deb persisted. "I mean, he had a regular voice, right? Maybe he wasn't a deceased spirit at all. Maybe you just thought that he was."

"Yes," I admitted. "I thought that way for a while. I assumed that I would be able to find the man. I figured for a time, even, that the phone calls were part of some elaborate prank played on me by one of my co-workers. I worked in a publications building. The administration building across the road was connected to the same phone system. So, for a while, I figured that the calls might have come from inside one of the buildings from one of my co-workers. So, I asked everyone I knew there who might have the voice range to fake such a call, posing as an old Indian gentleman. But when I quizzed them, people would just look me in the eye and shake their heads in wonder. You can tell when people are trying to trick you, if you stare into their eyes. That was not the case.

"I even asked the switchboard operator if she had transferred calls from such a man, routing them to me. She said no. So it appears that the man called my extension without asking to be routed. He sought me out."

"But I still don't understand how you can be sure that he was dead, a ghost," Deb said.

"Well, his talk about meditation training got me to thinking. I had a sudden urge to go downstairs to our bookstore and look through books that offered meditation training. You might say that I was directed or even driven. Maybe it was just a hunch, but I felt moved to go to one certain book shelf. I immediately found a book there on meditation technique with back cover copy about its author who directed people to meditate in the early morning light beside water outdoors. The book cover copy said that he also was famous for leading lighting rod tours of India in the early fall. The author was an old mystic from India who had died shortly before that book's printing. That fit my caller perfectly to a T."

"Wow," Deb said.

"Yeah, goose bumps," I agreed. "I got actual chills when I saw that book and figured it out. That man had called me from the spirit realm to tell me about the transformative powers of natural light. He wanted me to know that we can move in the light as light beings, free of the limitations of the dense, physical world and the bodies that encompass us. He wanted me to know that our higher self can move about freely in the light, beyond space and time. And, to be sure, death had no hold on him. Death had no significance for him. He was a free spirit."

"Hmm," Deb pondered. "Well, you know, I was in a fire once. Well, it wasn't much of a fire, as it turned out. At the time, though, I thought it might be the end. I didn't rise up out of my body or suspend time and space in that emergency. I just thought to myself, sick as I was at the time, that it might be a speedier death than slowly rotting away with cancer. Maybe that was wrong of me; but that's what I thought at the time."

"And now you don't feel that way, right?" I said.

"I have something to live for. I have hope. Tomorrow will be brighter. Now I have my whole life in front of me."

I was taken back at her openness in revealing to me, a stranger, her innermost doubts and dark thoughts. I just stared into my empty tea cup.

"But I see what you're saying," Deb said finally. "Maybe it's an illusion that we are trapped by our rotting bodies. I mean, everyone is slowly dying, right? Eventually our bodies will decay with age, if nothing else. So if we think of life as only physical form, then life seems short and terminal. But maybe we can live outside our bodies – even better lives."

I nodded my head and looked up from the cup.

"That man on the phone convinced me that death as we commonly know it does not exist. It has no hold on us."

"And your book will describe how to move freely in the light – show how to do it?" she asked me.

"I will try," I said. "I want to make it personal, so people can relate to it – not just a meditation *how-to* book."

62

We talked a little bit more about my including examples of elephants, whales, and birds. Yes, it did seem a stretch. But I couldn't look around me and find any better examples of living creatures who lived in harmony with nature, spirit, and light. These pure souls lived in the light every day. They were in sync with nature. Other than that, I had just the example of a dead guy that I claimed had called me on the telephone. Some people might find that hard to believe.

Looking closely at Deb, I thought that she believed me. After all, she had been to edge of physical death herself and returned, now revitalized. She didn't look at anything quite the same anymore.

I looked at Deb and saw a young woman who desperately wanted to escape the physical restrictions of a body to move about freely, far beyond the four walls around her.

As she gathered up the cups and brought them to the kitchen sink, I thanked her for the tea. She thanked me for sharing.

Chapter 3
March-June 1992

Deb fully settled into our old, Victorian house with the witch's cap on top by mid-March. In fact, she called the place "our wonderful house." She seemed comfortable at home there with me, along with a couple of other house mates who never seemed to be home, and seven territorial cats – two of hers and five of mine. I had inherited some of my feline roommates from previous owner and caterer Georgia Affett, when some of her cats refused to go into crates to ship off to San Antonio, Texas with her.

Deb loved the cats and cared for all of them when I was away. Occasionally I would disappear for a few days on book presentations or book fairs for Llewellyn Publications. Deb kept my old Aloe Vera plants happy and the cats in a harmonious state of co-existence. She had a gentle way about her.

On the other hand, I could see that she was home-bound a lot, worked long hours for little reward, and didn't seem to have many outside friends. She would disappear in a flash in the morning wearing one of those Lancôme Paris blazers that dominated her closet and zip away for work in that little, red puddle jumper of a car.

When she would come home a little late from work, my first reaction was that she would get together with friends for a couple hours at the end of the day. She was seldom that late coming home. Apparently, she had a couple of friends from work, both women about her age who worked in the same part of the same store. It was a large shopping center, but a small corner within the shopping center where Deb and her friends worked.

It took me a while to determine that a lot of time Deb would come home a little late after working extra hours to set out sale merchandise, settle her department's cash-out report at the end of her shift, and prepare sale signs and markdowns for the next day. Frankly, I believe a lot of that extra work might have been off the clock, as though anything more than the $6.85 or so the department store chain paid her to manage the department without the rank of manager might somehow break them. But I came to recognize that Deb Bennett was a young woman who took her responsibilities very seriously.

She would grab some sort of snacks from our kitchen after work and plop herself into her deep wicker rocking chair in front of the television. Sometimes she would open up and blurt out the names of her co-workers, which seemed to be about the only people left in her life. One of them worked in the cosmetic counter with her, but hadn't been there as long as Deb. While Deb was asked to take responsibility as department manager without the title, it only mean more work for Deb. She complained that her co-worker in the cosmetic counter got to wear a lab coat and go behind the scenes to where the cosmetics came together. It was easy to see how that bothered Deb and conflicted her relationship with one of her few friends there.

The Roseville shopping center where they worked was part of a trendy bedroom community just up the road from where we lived in Saint Paul. Many of Saint Paul's stores were relocating there. Many of our people were moving there, too. It was more upscale, rich, and white. Deb couldn't have afforded to live in the community where she worked, most likely. The house where we lived was only five miles or so south of there. In the inner city where we lived, gunshots rang out in the night; and drug deals went down in front of our house. The sign placed by the city on our street, declaring it to be a "Drug Free Zone" didn't seem to deter anyone.

Deb invited me to come see where she worked. I think she was proud of those red Lancôme blazers and the fact she ran the cosmetics counter at a major, upscale department store. I was afraid that I'd get cornered into one of those make-overs, if I dropped by at a slack time when they might want to create some excitement at their kiosk. So, when I did visit the store, I went at a busy time on a busy day. Or so I thought.

Deb was looking at something in the display case when I got there. She was alone at the counter. She had no customers, not even browsers. Altogether, the big department store was pretty dead. I guess I didn't know key shopping hours or the habits of mall shoppers.

The area where she worked had a glass counter that wrapped around her. She sat on a stool in the center, with all sorts of cosmetics and bright, shiny collectables in the display area under glass counters. The tops of the glass counters also held some items that were highlighted with promotional signs. I recognized Deb's writing on some of the sale signs. Her style of sign-making included a combination of handwriting and printing, with large, rounded letters that were tall and full. It was the handwriting of a person who was open and genuine, not holding anything back. I wondered how a person who had been riddled with brain cancer much of her young life and lost her family could be so brave and forthcoming.

She looked up from the sale item that she was cradling in her hands.

"Oh!" she said, standing up quickly. "You came after all."

"You seem surprised?" I said.

"Well, a little. I mean, a cosmetic counter. Young women and women who want to look young drop by here for make-overs. They're looking for some sort of magic in a box. There's not much for men here, really."

"I came to visit you and see where you work," I explained.

"Well, this is it," she said. "It's pretty much just me and the makeup. It's sorta slow this time of day, boring to sit here."

"Is it just you working?" I asked.

Deb pointed to an unmarked door down the aisle.

"My co-worker is in the back. She gets to wear the lab coat today. But that's okay. Nothing much happening here just now. Just sorta quiet, sitting here by myself."

I noticed how Deb primped to come to work every day. Her hair was perfect. Her clothes were pressed. She was wearing makeup, as though going out to a ball. Or at least that's the way it struck me. It seemed like a lot of effort to come to work here and spend hours on your feet, waiting on people who mostly just wanted a free make-over.

"You always wear that red blazer for work?" I asked.

"Yup," she said. "It's like a uniform. One of our suppliers provides them. I have several."

I noticed that she had worn a hat to work but set it aside.

"Hard hat area?" I joked, pointing at her stylish hat.

"That's my look," Deb said. "I gotta have my hat."

"I've never seen you wear one before," I said.

"Just when I walk into the store," she said, "to set the stage."

"So, do you validate?" I asked.

"Validate what?" she said.

"Parking," I said. "left my car on one of those parking levels. I only hope that I can find it again. There are so many cars parked here at the mall. I'll probably walk out the wrong door and get all turned around."

"Never lose your car," she advised. "I love my little, red car."

I smiled and waved, leaving her to preside over her trinkets and potions in solitude. She seemed so bored, so alone. Where was the joy for a miraculous cancer survivor to grab life with both hands in triumph?

I thought about nothing but that on the short drive home and decided to make her a spaghetti dinner. It wasn't much, but something I did on occasion to brighten the day.

Deb didn't come home on time, but mysterious appeared a couple of hours later. She didn't seem hungry but made herself some special coffee she'd collected on the way home. It was a foreign blend and freshly ground. The aroma was overwhelming. Yes, that was one way to warm up the day.

She sat in her wicker chair and just sipped her coffee, missing Star Trek on the television. I could see how she stayed so thin. Just coffee for dinner and then buzzing around all day. We laughed that anything could make her miss a Star Trek rerun classic, but still she was cryptic about where she'd been.

"I do really like Star Trek," said the mystery woman. "No matter how messed up things get there on the Enterprise, they always work it out in the end. It's like those people have evolved and learned how to get along. There is no need for money. Everybody gets to follow their dreams. They are all so brave and explore the darkness of space without fear. I would like to be there, on the Enterprise. Who wouldn't?"

I told her that I was nowhere near that brave and adventurous and would get scared to death to go into outer space at any time.

She laughed.

"What about the old Indian man?" she chided. "What would he say to you?"

I was stumped. "What do you mean?" I asked.

"Well, wasn't that the guy who encouraged you to go on a trip to India and said it would change your life forever if you went?" she said. "That guy."

"Hey, maybe it was Captain Kirk," I quipped.

"William Shatner is a Canadian, not from India," she reminded me.

One of her cats – an old, fluffy black tom cat, walked up to her and just sat beside her wicker chair.

"Wizard!" she said and deftly lifted herself out of the chair to kneel down beside him. The old, long-haired black cat stood proudly beside her and remained still, as she gently stroked him from his forehead all the way down to the tip of his tail.

"He's been with me through thick and thin, you know" Deb said. "He's my little guardian angel."

I remarked how well he got along with the other cats but was nonetheless a loner.

"Oh, he'll disappear for hours at a time, and I won't even know where he is," she said. "But when I need to see him, he's right there by my side. He's magical."

Deb crawled on the old, green living room carpet to the wicker basket that held all of her cat toys. She searched until she found something long and dangling. It looked like an old, white shoelace.

"He loves playing with me," she said of the cat. "He doesn't play so much with the other cats, though. He just sits with them and cares for the younger ones. But he likes our little games."

Still on her knees, Deb held the white shoelace over the cat's head and started to circle it around and around in a teasing sort of way. The cat responded by swiping at the line, but only when it had rounded his head and came around to circle in front of him. They had worked out a sort of rhythm and a ritualistic manner of playing together.

Soon the old cat tired of the game and walked a few feet from her to plop down, looking at her with soft eyes. He blinked, like a sort of cat code that might say something like, 'I'm totally comfortable in your presence and spending my time with you.'

Deb held the shoelace over the wicker basket and then dropped it. The cat seemed mesmerized to see the length of it disappear little by little, as it fell.

"I need to get him a pretty pink ribbon to play this game right," Deb said. "I need my ribbons for a project I'm doing now, but I'll probably have leftover scraps for him one of these days soon."

I asked her about the project that required pink ribbon. She seemed a little slow to answer.

"Oh, I like to work with little craft projects in my room - needle and thread stuff. Nothing big. It's just something to keep me busy."

"I hear your stereo and TV when you're in your room," I said. "It never occurred to me that you were sewing or whatever in there at same time."

Deb shrugged. "Something to keep my hands busy."

I looked at her hands. She had long, thin fingers, the kind you might expect to see on a pianist who could stretch out and reach all of the right keys. I also could detect a nervous twitch in her hands. It seemed totally understandable that she might be uptight after all of her illness and the loss of her son and husband.

"And I collect teddy bears," she added. "Special stuffed bears. You know the Coca-Cola Bears? That's what I like. I have only a few but would love to get some more."

I looked blank and shook my head, as though I knew nothing about these collectables.

"I can show you a couple, if you want," Deb said. She sprang to her feet and her full six-foot height. She lead the way through the living room past the dining room with the parquet floor and up the staircase to the top floor. At the top of the stairs, she turned right and walked the length of the upstairs hallway to her room at the end.

The room was very familiar to me, as it had been my first bedroom there at the old Victorian house. As part of the old attic, remodeled in the 1970s sometime, the room had strange ceilings of various heights and odd bends to the room. The room was basically L-shaped. When you came in the bedroom door, there was a pop-out door to the remaining crawl space dead ahead of you, with most of the remaining room angled to the left.

Most people, including me and now Deb, put their beds against the far wall in the elongated part of the room, although the low ceiling in that part of the room made it tricky getting in and out of bed. The room to the left ended with a couple of windows that overlooked the muddy back yard. This back yard had once been Ramsey Park that apparently had a pond, now reduced to muddy ground. Around the corner in Deb's bedroom was a clothes closet. The upstairs bathroom was on the other side of the back of her closet.

The room's decor was drab dry wall that was never painted beyond the original white primer. The carpet was that old, green carpet from decades past, much like the living room. I had tried to patch the carpet that was frayed and tattered at the door frame and elsewhere in the house, where cats had clawed under closed doors to try to gain passage. My patch on Deb's bedroom carpet at the door frame resembled a small map of Montana.

When I moved into that bedroom a year ago, I had replaced a depressed young woman who slept most of the day on a thin mattress on the floor and yelled if anyone disturbed her. I was worried when I toured the room to consider moving there, after hearing that she had thrown coffee into the face of the landlady's handyman. He'd made the mistake of knocking on her door one afternoon without response and then entering the room. But the landlady was glad to turn the room and also turn her out, when I agreed to live there.

Months later, when the house became available with Georgia Affett's decision to take a job in Texas, I was relieved to move out of this cramped, dismal bedroom and move into the master bedroom at the other end of the hall. So, I felt sorry that I didn't have a better room to offer Deb.

She seemed to like it there in that little, colorless room, however. She had her stereo on the wall opposite her bed and her television set up near the door. She had set up a small table with a hardback chair near the windows. I saw that she had put up a makeup mirror on the table, near her clothes closet. And there were books here and there.

But the Coca-Cola Bears were the real show stopper. She had arranged them as honored guests on her bed and propped them against the wall, as a sort of welcoming committee to anyone who entered the room. At last, I understood.

These were stuffed teddy bear versions of the animated bears that had appeared in the Coca-Cola Christmas ads. I wasn't much into teddy bears, but I could understand the warmth and homespun happiness that these cozy Christmas bears projected.

"See!" she said, pointing them out. She picked one up and straightened its little Santa cap on top. "Coca-Cola Bears that look just like the Christmas bears. I would love to find some more. I heard there's a new one every year. They are numbered by the year they come out"

She handed me one of the bears. Yes, it had a year on it, so collectors could identify which year it had been issued. It would be great to have a full set. I wanted to get her one but had no idea where they came from.

"I'll keep my eye out for you," I promised. "Maybe in my travels I'll come across one."

"That would be great," she said. "They're hard to find."

I told her that I was going to Florida where I liked to take vacations. I thought about the big Swap Shop at Fort Lauderdale, a huge flea market, circus and produce stand that sprawled across an immense lot that had once been home to several drive-in movie screens. One drive-in screen remained, but the rest of the huge lot was now used by the Swap Shop. They had everything from tools to watches.

"That would be great," she said. "You see the ones I have. Look for ones from different years, if you can."

And so, I prepared for my annual vacation to Lauderdale-by-the-Sea, a seaside strip of small, family-owned motels just across the road from public beaches. I discussed feeding the cats and garbage pickup days with Deb. She also agreed to water my old Aloe-Vera plants. There were so many cats with different eating programs. Some went outside, and some did not.

And, on top of that, I felt sorry about leaving Deb alone in that big house so soon after welcoming her there. Honestly, I felt guilty that she had never been anywhere outside the state, except to work as a grocery store clerk briefly in Texas. She looked too excited to hear about my trip – and frankly a little jealous.

But I had earned two weeks of vacation, working a year at Llewellyn in Saint Paul, and figured now was a good time to take one of those weeks. There were plenty of book fairs, trade shows, sales calls, and deadlines ahead; so now was a good time for me to get away. So, I packed a bag and booked a motel room with a kitchen. I got a little rental car, a Metro that could barely maintain highway speeds. But I was bound for Florida, with a few days to spend on the beach and time out for an all-day adventure to the big Swap Shop nearby.

I resisted the urge to call the house in Saint Paul, even though we had a house phone back then. I figured that things would go alright for Deb, the cats, and the plants. It's just that a vacation is a time when a guy needs to disconnect. But reclining on the beach, I felt the urge to get myself out to the Swap Shop and see what I could find. The place had everything, even Christmas gifts. And maybe I could even find a Coca-Cola Bear or two for Deb.

Driving the baby Metro car proved dangerous. I was almost blown off the highway with trucks that passed me. And then, parking at the Swap Shop, I forgot that there was a short divider that blocked the front of my Metro from the parking stall directly in front of me. Granted, most cars could probably just drive over it without incident; but the little Metro found the divider too high to negotiate safely, and I scraped the oil pan. I worried all the time I was at the Swap Shop – pretty much all day, given all that there was to see. But even worrying about a possible leak from the creased oil pan, I was unwilling to hurry my all-day adventure into the massive Swap Shop.

After taking in the indoor circus in the food emporium and hitting all the fruit stands with bags of oranges and avocados to carry home, I walked through all of the aisles with a seemingly endless supply of designer-copy watches, all priced at $8 including free extra bands and batteries. Then I saw all of the new gadgets with live demonstrations, craft items, island imports, and tools. There was so much to see; and my bags were getting full.

At last, in the back in the open-air part of the Swap Shop, I found the used collectables. At last, I found a booth that had teddy bears. There were so many teddy bears; and they all looked a little worn and dirty. There were a couple of Coca-Cola Bears and other bears that were dressed pretty much like the Coca-Cola Bears. I regret to this day that I opted for a couple of newer teddy bears that resembled Christmas bears, but were not actually Coca-Cola Bears.

They were hard to tell apart, except that the copies of the Coca-Cola Bears did not have years on them. And I saved maybe ten or twenty dollars. Shrewd. So, I guess I did know the difference, but figured Deb wouldn't much care. That was so silly of me, of course, looking back on it today. A collector, after all, is precisely focused on what she collects.

After my walk through the entire Swap Shop, I doubled back to the opening where stalls offered all of the incredible fruit and vegetables. There were oranges as big as grapefruit and avocados as large as cantaloupe. And toward the end of the long shopping day, many fruit vendors were marking down what was left and offering generous samples to entice buying. I had watermelon, honeydew melon, and peach samples. Unfortunately, I could carry home no more bags, as the car was still several yards away.

But out of the corner of one eye, I did see something that seemed a little out of place in a fruit and vegetable stand. They were large necklaces of beautiful jade. The green stones glistened in the late afternoon sun, peeking through the awnings. I moved closer in fascination at the size of the stones strung together in what must be called crude construction. The jade was not precisely cut or polished. The stones were natural shards of semi-precious stones of immense honest beauty. And they were all attractively priced at $15 and $20 apiece.

I thought about Deb never going anywhere exotic and her secret love of beauty. I pointed to one of the large necklaces, which proved fairly heavy once it was handed to me. I questioned whether anyone would honestly wear it, due to its weight and size and the sharp edges of the unrefined stones. Deb was particularly slender and fair, so I didn't see her really wearing such a necklace. But I did think that she would like it. So, I wrapped in around one arm and trudged the many yards back to my rented Metro.

The oil pan on the little Metro wasn't leaking after my earlier parking mishap, so I loaded up the little car and sputtered my way back home as fast as the little wind-up car could manage.

In a couple of days when I wrapped up my Florida vacation and returned home, I snuck the jade necklace and Christmas bears into the house, hidden in bags.

Deb met me at the door with some tale about a strange woman named Georgia Affett who claimed to be the former landlady of our Victorian house. It seems that Georgia had showed up quite unannounced during my week away and said that I'd told her she could stay at the house while undergoing a trial in Saint Paul.

I felt sorry for Georgia. She was forced to give up her catering business shortly before selling me the house, after a car had slammed into her while she was loading the back end of a van with catered food early one morning. She was trying to collect for long-term physical damage that demonstrated hard to prove, since the injury involved soft tissue damage that left her feeling fatigued, despite looking healthy on the outside. Apparently, soft tissue damage is hard to prove medically.

On top of her medical and legal problems, Georgia was finding her move to San Antonio to be financially difficult, since her wages in the right-to-work state were far less than she had expected. With the money from the sale of her Saint Paul duplex to me, she was only able to afford a small condo; and she was finding that expensive to maintain with association dues and upgrades. With all of her money problems, my old landlady had taken the man who ran into her to court to try to collect whatever damages she could.

Georgia had thought she could sleep on the living room sofa at the home that she had recently owned and operated as landlady. I'm sure she thought that I would be most sympathetic to her, having lived with her at the house. She probably thought I owed her one, too, after the low-ball price I exacted from her in order to buy her three-story Victorian house. What she hadn't figured was my absence when she flew into town for her court date.

Deb was dying to tell me all about Georgia's visit and all of the amazing things that Georgia had to say; but I urged Deb first to look over some things that I had purchased in Florida. After I had dropped most of my bags in front of my bedroom door, I turned to Deb with the remaining two bags – one paper and one plastic. She looked curious. There's nothing like closed bags that hold potential treasures to create some interest. So, I toyed with her a little, the way she might toy with one of her cats.

"Betcha wonder what I got in these bags, right? Got your interest?"

Her smile beamed, and eyes widened.

"Let's go into your room to see where it will all fit," I teased.

She led the way down the hall and opened the door. Inside the room, I extended both arms, each one holding a bag of mystery.

"Well, I'll let you decide which one of these you want," I said.

She pointed to the larger of the two bags I held.

I opened the plastic bag and pulled out two Christmas bears. After doing that, I looked over at her bed to see how well they matched up with her Coca Cola bears. They didn't. I felt bad immediately.

"At the Florida Swap Shop, I found your teddy bears," I said. "There were several to choose from. I thought these looked the best and hoped they would fit in with your collection. Want them?"

I was a disappointed in her outward reaction. She didn't seem all that excited.

She reached out to touch them but showed only a small smile.

"They're nice," she said. "Thank you."

"Or," I said, "you can choose bag number two here." I held out the paper bag, still closed.

She cocked her head to one side, as though perplexed.

I opened the bag for her and handed her the large jade necklace.

Her smile widened, and eyes bulged.

"Wow!" she said. "Is this real jade?"

"Yes," I said. "Caribbean. There are many items from the Caribbean islands and areas near the south Florida coast. "Anyway, I thought you might like the necklace, although it's probably too big to actually wear."

She nodded her head and placed the necklace around her stereo by the door.

"It looks good there," she said. "I love it."

"Well, I thought of you when I saw it. So, I brought a little bit of Florida and the Caribbean Islands to you."

I pointed to the teddy bears.

"Those are yours, too, of course. I was just teasing you about having to choose, being a bit dramatic."

"That's very sweet of you," she said. "I love them all."

Nonetheless, I felt that it wasn't enough. I waved one hand at the open doorway.

"Hey, let's get some tea; and you can tell me about Georgia's visit!" I suggested.

Downstairs, Deb took charge of the tea pot. As she bustled around the kitchen, I sat down alone at the table in the kitchenette.

"Well!" she began, eager to tell her story, "I was pretty surprised when she turned up at the door with that story. Georgia....was that her name?"

"Yup," I replied. "Georgia Affett. She owned the house before me. She was my landlady here."

"Right! That's what she told me. Then she said you had told her it was okay for her to stay here during her trial. She told me about the accident and her deep tissue injuries."

"Well, we might have discussed her staying her at some point," I said. "I don't exactly recall those words, but it's okay. Sorry she surprised you like that. I mean, you didn't know her from Adam. It was pretty trusting of you to let her in and let her sleep here."

"Well, I figured that's what you would have wanted," Deb said. "I didn't know. But she seemed so certain about everything."

"That's Georgia," I said. "You should have seen her drilling us on how best to clean the house on Saturdays. She takes charge."

"It was okay," Deb said. She seemed nice. I don't think she's happy with her new job in Texas or happy about moving away from here, though. And then she has those nagging injuries with no way to pay her doctor bills. She can't even get her insurance to cover it, because they don't see anything wrong. And the doctors don't really think she's hurting."

"Well, do you know how her court case came out?"

"No. I don't think anything much came of it. I think it was against the driver, not the insurance company."

"How was she otherwise," I asked.

"She wishes she wouldn't have moved, wishes she wouldn't have sold the house."

"So, you had quite a talk with her," I said.

"Yeah," Deb said.

"How are her cats?" I asked. "Bet they don't like living in a condo. And did she see Mister K when she was here? That was her top cat, but he refused to go into a crate and hid when she left. She called him Kitten. But I renamed him Mister K, since he's so big and dominant."

"Yeah, she saw K. I think he remembered her. But she thinks the house stinks now with so many cats here."

"Oh, that's rich!" I said. "There were more cats when she lived here. She had five. I had one and then got two more. Another renter had two. She lives with three cats now in a small condo."

"She said it was the litter boxes," Deb said. "She said the cats need more boxes or else the boxes need to be cleaned more often. I think she's probably right. Cats settle into a place, and they get territorial. I can see what she means."

"Okay, we can work on that," I said. "I guess it's true that her cats are all related, while our cats here are all strangers, trying to co-exist in a strange house."

"We'll work it out," Deb said, pouring some of her curious tea. "We have lots of time to work these things out."

Chapter 4
July-August 1992

As the summer moved on, I found myself making more business trips for the publishing house, often taking off for days at a time. During my absences, Deb excelled at caring for our houseful of cats. Not all of them seemed to co-exist harmoniously together in the Victorian house, as Deb and I had initially believed, and one or two of them waged silent, but fragrant territorial battles here and there. We needed to keep bottles to spray down favorite doors and walls wherever they marked their territory. We had another bottle that was supposed to discourage them from marking with urine where it was sprayed, but I don't think the cats much believed in the power of that bottle.

So, while I was gone, Deb had her hands full at home, trying her luck at cat herding – an impossible challenge. But she was game. And that probably prevented her from having much of a social life or any sort of life outside the home, except to report to work at the department store's cosmetic counter five or six days each week.

During this summer, in the days when I would be home for any stretch of time, I did take notice of a feral cat who was attempting to hang out in a side storage shed among the rakes, shovels, and lawn equipment outside. This cat was very skittish, probably abandoned or abused to the point where people seemed like something to be avoided.

Deb noticed me sneaking out to the area near the shed one morning to leave food and water for the feral cat. She stood under the covered porch, watching me try to position the food and water out of the summer rain. She watched quietly.

The problem was that I could not get the cat to come near me. It must have been severely mistreated by someone in the neighborhood. Perhaps they had neglected it so badly that it left its home. Or maybe they kicked it out or abandoned it to live by its own devices. I know that some people in our neighborhood abandoned their cats when they moved; and local family evacuations in the challenging economy had been horrendous lately. After all, this was the inner city.

What was most evident in looking at this shy cat who tried its best to seek shelter under my leaking, old shed was that it was so badly malnourished. It was thin and discolored from lack of proper nutrition. As far as I could tell, it was supposed to be an orange and white cat. But the orange in his fur was so discolored that it appeared faint.

Also, this poor cat was terribly thin, and it probably needed medical attention. I really wanted to help him, but he wouldn't let me near him.

So, when I put the food and water inside the shed to avoid the rain, he would vacate the shed. My dilemma was that I could either keep the food dry from the rain or put the food outside the shed, as I usually did, to keep the frightened cat inside the shed and dry.

I settled with leaving the food and water inside the shed and decided that the cat would return to the shelter as soon as I left. One evening after setting down his food and watching him flee, I was standing on the front porch, dripping wet.

"Well, you tried," Deb told me as she joined me under the covered porch. "That poor thing is just afraid of people, I think. It's not you. I'm sure it appreciates you giving him food. Somebody else ruined his little life.

"Come on inside," she said. "You need to dry off."

I raced up the stairs to the upper duplex part of the house where we lived, with Deb behind me. Once inside, I plopped down on the sofa in the living room, shivering from the rain dripping from my hair.

Deb brought me a towel from the bathroom and handed it to me.

"Oh, thanks," I said, quickly running it across my wet head. "That's exactly what I needed. What I didn't need was that summer rain. The downpours seem to come out of nowhere. But that's typical of the Midwest, I suppose."

"You know," Deb said, "That cat might never warm up to you. If it's been badly mistreated and no longer trusts people, it might never let you near it."

I looked at her a long time, trying to figure out what she expected me to say.

"Well," I finally said, "I can live with that. I can continue feeding it outside and maybe improve the shed so that it doesn't leak. Maybe I could even winterize it, so the cat could live there comfortably even in cold weather. I mean, I have to try the best I can. It has no place else to go. What else can I do?"

She nodded. "It probably needs to see a vet," she said. "It probably needs to be vaccinated. It needs to be checked for worms. And it's dirty, matted, and needs to be cleaned up."

I looked downward, lost in thought. It occurred to me that simply feeding and providing decent shelter for the cat at the shed would give it some sense of hope. Maybe it would feel loved and begin cleaning itself again. Scampering around without anyone to care for it, the cat probably didn't even have time to clean itself properly. And I could see that it had no remaining pride, abandoned and neglected as it was.

From that day forward, I started a feeding schedule for the feral cat at the shed, bringing it fresh food and water every morning at dawn and every evening at dusk. I tried to make my feedings scheduled as close to the same time each day as possible. I began putting over-the-counter worming medicine into its food every few days, just in case it had parasitic round worm issues.

Working around the times of the day when the cat would be away from the shelter, I started improving the shed by adding extra boards topped with roofing material to make it more rainproof. Fortunately, I had some roofing material left over from the house; it even matched the house and looked like it belonged.

I found some pieces of left-over insulation in the attic and lined the inner walls to the shed, covering over that with plastic. With a new door and cat flap, it was almost habitable. Only I couldn't get the cat used to using the cat flap. I left the door part way open and later tried removing the plastic flap from the little cat door at the bottom of the door.

Try as I would, however, the cat did not warm up to me. It backed off or simply ran away when I approached with food and water. On days when I was late coming home or rushed to get to work, Deb would put out food and water for the discolored orange and white cat. And Deb always gave me a progress report with the encouraging news that the cat was letting her get closer at feeding time. Apparently, she had better luck than I did. The cat was warming up to her.

I was leaving for several days at a time now, as the major book fairs were all scheduled during the long summer months. Deb always watered my indoor plants and outside flower beds and also cared for all of the critters in our old Victorian house during these absences. Added to her extra duties was the care of the feral cat by the side of our house, of course.

Honestly, it never occurred to me to pay her for all of that tender loving care during my business trips, but I really should have done so. It must have taken her close to an hour every morning and every evening to water and feed everything at the house.

One of my final trade shows of the summer was the Canadian Booksellers' Association annual book fair. It was only three days, but the trip was closer to a week when I needed to account for time to set up the booth, secure lodging and a car, and then disassemble the booth at the end.

As before with my Miami trip, I could tell that Deb was jealous about all of my travel. To me it was just work. To her, it would have been a unique opportunity to escape and see some of the outside world. As she kept reminding me, she'd never been anywhere and really wanted some adventure now that she had recovered from her cancer.

I returned from Canada with a box of Canadian candy for Deb. It was not an imaginative or elaborate gift, but I felt like I should bring a little bit of the outside world to her, if she was unable to see it on her own. It was a small brick of Scottish toffee, as I recall.

Deb told me that she had met someone, a young man who was actually younger than she was. I wondered just how young he was, since her son in Minneapolis was about twelve years old. I had never met her son Jamie, since she apparently no longer had custody of him.

Nor did I meet the young boyfriend.

"I never thought that I could go out with someone who smoked!" Deb told me. "I never have and thought that I never would."

Her views on smoking took me back, as I smoked a pipe in the house and never thought much about it. Yes, there was the stink from the smoking, but also a real health concern for second-hand smoke. Somebody who had made a full recovery from brain cancer wanted a healthy life style. Consistent with that, Deb ate healthy food and had white teeth that smokers would envy.

"This guy smokes!" Deb repeated. "I decided that it was okay. I could live with that."

I was fond of Deb, but really not jealous. I loved being her friend and house mate but could not ever consider us a couple. There was a difference in age. Also, it seemed like a conflict of interest with her as my renter. And besides all that, I was a little intimidated by the whole idea of a brain tumor – even though hers had cleared up.

I kept thinking about a charming, young woman that I had known years ago in Mount Vernon, Washington. I met her when we both worked for the newspaper there. What held me back from knowing her better was her health. She told me that she had a brain tumor and was undergoing treatment. Even though she indicated the treatment was going well, I could not get the idea out of my mind that her head was a ticking time bomb and could explode at any minute. I didn't want to be there when that happened.

Deb, the miraculous cancer survivor, meanwhile charted her romantic possibilities with this young man she'd just met. She told me how sweet and considerate he was and how he took her out to dinner. I was very happy for her. Her new life was slowly beginning to unfold; and it could be beautiful.

She was so giddy with happiness, in fact, that she didn't even complain about cat litter boxes and the smell of cats during my absence. I'm certain that my territorial tom cats had sprayed the furniture, doors, and kick boards in the hallways, as they generally did to act out their frustration and disapproval when I was away for more than a day. But Deb was all smiles when I returned and reported no household problems.

I went for a jog down at Como Park on the nature trails there at dusk on my first day back from Canada. I wondered whether Deb might be interested in jogging or at least a nature walk. I had never asked her.

Back home that night, I found her in front of the TV in her wicker rocker, swinging back and forth, as she watched a Star Trek rerun intently. She'd discovered where to find the original episodes from the Sixties. She was in another world, absorbed in the program, so I went upstairs to change clothes after my jog. Really, I didn't even feel that she noticed me walking upstairs, as her eyes remained glued to the TV set only two feet in front of her.

When I returned to the living room, I figured we might have an end-of-day chat, if her television program had ended. Only she wasn't there. I went to the kitchen, but didn't see her there, either. Neither was she in the laundry room. I considered that she might be in her bedroom, so began to sit down in the living room myself and await her return.

I sat quietly for a while and then heard the front door open. I figured it might be one of our elusive other house mates that we rarely saw. But I heard Deb's voice from the bottom of the front stairs.

"Come see what I found for you!" she called up to me.

When I walked down the stairs, I noticed that the front door was still ajar, but without Deb standing there. So, I pushed the door open and walked onto the front porch. She was not on the porch by the door, either, however.

"Down here!" she called. "Come down here and see what I found for you!"

I couldn't believe my eyes. Deb had the feral orange and white cat in her arms. It wasn't struggling or apparently even scared. It rested gently in her arms.

"I think his name should be Peaches," she said. "The orange in his fur is pretty faded, but he does look like a peach, don't you think?"

The cat was so neglected that it was hard to tell whether he was just dirty or faint in his coloration. The orange was very indistinct. So was his white fur. He was covered with dust and tangles.

"He's badly malnourished," Deb pronounced. "He'll clean up pretty well, once you take a brush to him and get him on a proper diet. And he should see a vet."

"He likes you," I said, "but I don't think he'll let me hold him."

"Oh, sure!" she said. "Look, I'll introduce you."

Deb deftly moved the cuddling cat nearer to me.

"Here is your cat, Peaches," she said. "Peaches, this is Von who will take good care of you now."

And then she simply handed the cat to me.

He made himself limp and pliable, but with a certain trepidation.

In just a moment, the discolored cat was resting easily in my arms, as it had in Deb's arms. I noticed that he didn't move a muscle or even twitch.

"You two were just made for each other," Deb said. "Let's take your new cat inside."

The three of us trudged up the front stairs very easily. I sat on the living room sofa with Peaches, who meekly let me pet him.

There was no talk of too many cats or male cats being territorial and a problem indoors. Deb had bridged the impossible very simply.

I took my eyes off the timid cat just long enough to catch Deb beaming at us.

"See how easy it can be?" she said. "He needed a home; and you love cats."

"But how did you get him to let you pick him up," I asked. "You made it seem so easy."

"Oh, I've been working at it, a little at a time, gaining his trust," she said. "Then I just asked him
98

if he would like to have a new home and would like to live inside with us. The choice was his."

She walked to the hallway closet and removed a cardboard box – one she'd used for moving her things into the house, and also a blanket from the overhead shelf. With her height, she could stand flat-footed and examine the entire contents of the overhead shelf, which she did to determine if there was a better choice than the blanket tucked under one arm.

Deb set the box in a corner near Wizard's wicker toy crate and folded the blanket to fit the box dimensions perfected. There were three layers of blanket for the new cat by the way she folded it.

"There's his bed," she announced. "Should we see if he's comfortable there? He might need to hide in a closet on his first day here, if he's not comfortable out here."

Just then, Deb's cat Mr. Wizard came into the room and sleepily examined the box before sniffing his toy box. He looked up at the cat in my arms.

"Well, we can see how they get along, too," I said, carrying the stray cat to the cardboard box.

I put the cat gently into its box and petted it, sitting on the floor next to the box. I continued stroking the cat to comfort it.

The stray cat looked nervously at Wizard but did not bolt. Old Mr. Wizard moved slowly toward the box and then carefully touched noses with Peaches. Neither cat flinched but held steady.

"I think they already know each other pretty well," Deb said. "Wizard probably met him outside. He probably even convinced Peaches that we were okay to trust."

There was no denying the result.

Wizard slowly sauntered out of the room, as though to give the new cat some privacy to rest and become acclimated on his own.

Deb stood up and turned toward the kitchen.

"I feel like a cup," she said. "How 'bout a cup to celebrate? We can celebrate Peaches the Cat in his new home."

"Don't feel like tea just now," I said.

"Not tea," she said. "Coffee. Always celebrate the big moments with really good coffee."

I passed on the coffee.

She returned, cradling a huge mug.

She positioned herself with the full coffee cup carefully in her wicker rocker. I turned my head to her, still petting the cat in the box.

"Deb," I said, "do you ever think about the way the people on Star Trek de-materialized and then re-materialize in their transporter devices?"

"You mean, like one minute they're in the room, and the next minute they're somewhere else?"

I nodded.

"Sort of like time travel, don't you think?" I said. "I mean they are no longer in the same time and space."

"Well, yeah," she said. "Another place, anyway."

"Do you think we'll ever be able to do that – escape time and space?" I asked.

She flashed a bright smile and had a dreamy look about her.

"Well, they were right about those communication devices, right? I mean, those hand-held communicators they used on Star Trek. People now have cell phones to carry with them, even if they're a little bulky."

"You mean those big, white bricks that people lug around with them?" I countered.

"Yeah, big and bulky now, perhaps," Deb said. "But just wait. They will get smaller. I'll bet we end up with phone you can fit in the palm of your hand. Just like the communicators on Star Trek."

"You Trekkies," I teased.

"Trekkers," she countered. "Fans of Star Trek are called Trekkers."

"Wouldn't it be great to escape the here and now and re-materialize somewhere else, though?" I asked.

"I'll bet we can do that, too, one day," Deb said. "I wouldn't be a bit surprised."

I asked her about her cat Mr. Wizard and how he seemed to disappear and reappear out of nowhere. I asked her if her cat had that sort of magical ability.

"Oh, he even gets out of rooms that are locked," she said of him. "I don't know how he does it. Maybe that would explain it."

I told her a little more about the book I had been researching and hoped to write on time and time travel. I compared it to astral projection where the spirit or energy body leaves the body in heightened consciousness and escapes mundane time and space to roam freely.

"So, the body would be like a vessel that you could abandon?" Deb said. "How do you get back into the body?"

I told her that Native American dream walkers and Hindu Samadhi mystics seemed to go into a trance-like state and leave the body to move throughout time and space, and apparently had no trouble returning to the body.

"It's like a great adventure," she said. "Just like Star Trek."

"Really, there's nothing to hold you back, if the spirit within you longs to be free," I said. "Scientists and mystics alike are beginning to think of time as not being fixed or linear but looped in a way that turns back on itself. So, the past, present, and future are actually happening simultaneous. What makes it seem that we are stuck in the present is our focused attention on being here now. Also, we feel limited by the way we stay neatly tucked inside our bodies, with a restricted view of things. But the spirit inside you, your higher consciousness, can rise outside the physical body, free of these restrictions. As a free spirit, as pure energy, it is not limited by the physical laws that keep us grounded and fixed in time and space. Pure energy."

"They had an episode on Star Trek where they went forward or backward in time through a black hole," she said.

"Well, if the Star Trek people can do it, then we can do it, too - right? Someday, I mean. Don't you think it's possible?"

"But on Star Trek, the entire star ship and all of the people were moved physically somewhere in time," Deb said.

I smiled.

"I am thinking more about spirit bodies as pure energy rising out of the body," I said, "as opposed to material bodies that are dense and cannot move at the speed of light. See, you'd need to move at the speed of light to move forward or backward in time. You wouldn't need a worm hole, if your spirit could rise up and travel all on its own. And why can't it? It's pure energy, right?"

We talked a little about people sending thoughts across great distances and people with visions of the past or future in their consciousness. Suddenly, it didn't seem so far-fetched to either of us.

"Are you sure you don't want some of this special coffee?" Deb asked. It's Dowd Egbert, imported from Canada."

Chapter 5
August–September 1992

As that summer with Deb wore down, I finished with my national and regional book fairs and trade shows for the most part, but still had a couple of other big trips coming up. There were the sales presentations on my publisher's new line of books to make before groups of sales representatives in Canada and the UK. Also, I had to get ready for the fall international book fair in Frankfurt, Germany, that would take me out of the country for a week and a half.

I felt guilty about leaving Deb alone with all of the cats under her care for so long. Granted, the presentations to sales reps on the new line of books took me out of the country for only a few days, since the actual presentations could be done in one afternoon. But the trips sounded glamorous and were certainly to exciting destinations. Deb showed great excitement about these trips and seemed to live them vicariously with me. But I know she would have loved taking these adventures into remote places she had never been. I tried to think about what little gifts along the way might interest her.

With now eight cats in our Victorian house, there were a lot of routines to remember twice a day. All of our cats seemed to have distinct personalities and lifestyles, so we had to keep a number of different cat foods on hand and remember which cat liked which kind of food. Frankly, I had a hard time remembering to do it right every day; and six of the eight cats were mine.

Deb decided to go over this regimen before I left for the presentation to our Canadian sales representatives, just to make certain. She rocked methodically in her wicker rocking chair as she went through all the cats and what they liked in her head.

"Okay," she said. "Let's see if I have it right. There's Mister K, the big black and white cat who likes Purina chicken. Then there's Zeke, the gray Maine Coon, who likes Fancy Feast. Salvador Dali, the big black cat, will eat any kibble, but prefers beef liver with lots of juice. Sabastian is the Rose Point Siamese, and he likes Tender Vittles. Selena, Salvador's little sister, prefers Kibbles and Bits, but will eat Fancy Feast. Peaches will eat anything. And that's all of your cats, right?"

I nodded, quite impressed.

"And then my cats. Wizard gets along with everyone; but Willow still hides under my bed."

"Have you introduced him to Peaches?" I asked. "They're both insecure and feel new here. Maybe they could bond."

Deb seemed to like the idea, so I figured she'd have something new to occupy her time. And now we were up to four litter boxes in the house and cleaned all of them twice each day.

"I hardly recognize Peaches now," I said. "He has much more color. Before I couldn't tell for certain whether he was orange and white or simply dirty. That orange color is really coming out now."

The new cat, it must be said, was still very shy. It was beginning to feel somewhat comfortable around the other cats; but Deb and I were the only people who didn't scare him away.

"I think Peaches will get over his fear of people soon, too," I said. "I remember how Salvador would always hide in closets. And he was born here. Nobody abused him. He still hides sometimes."

"Salvador's a little crazy," Deb told me. "Not in a bad way. It's just the way he is. Everybody has their problems. He just feels vulnerable."

She stood up, apparently too soon, and had to catch her balance on the side arm of her wicker rocker.

"Are you alright?" I asked.

"Me?" she asked. "Yeah, but I think I might have a cold or something. Maybe it's a summer cold. I'll be alright."

"I hate to leave you with all of the cats and plants, if you're not feeling okay," I said.

"Naw," she said. "I'll be fine. I'll just take something, and I'll be fine."

I sort of put that out of my mind for the moment, only because there was so much packing to do and other aspects to getting ready for my trips. These book junkets might sound like fun travel but did involve a lot of work just getting ready and clearing my desk of routine business for the next few days. Then there was the hurry-up-and-go aspect to rushing to the airport and then arriving jet-lagged with set-up work at the other end as soon as I got there. Often, I would be exhausted before I actually got to the book shows and presentations. Then coming home, there would be plenty of work to process and routine day-to-day work that I would need to catch up on. Then there was all of the laundry to process and home maintenance to catch up on once I finally got back home. Then I'd usually need to catch up on sleep when I got home. Yes, I originally took my job with great excitement about all of the travel that I would do, but soon grew to almost dread the trips, especially when they followed each other so closely in the summer and fall.

Deb watched me pack with great interest, vicariously enjoying the anticipation of the trip and the adventures ahead. I would bump into her in the laundry; and she would insist that I go ahead of her in washing and drying my clothes to pack. To tell the truth, I never put that much planning or preparation into packing and often put off packing half of my things until the last

108

minute. I think she would have been a much better traveler.

All of the cats seemed to sense that I was taking off again and started to act nervous about my deserting them. Salvador Dali sprayed some of my clothes set out on the bed next to the suitcase. Little Selena tried hiding in the suitcase, and I found her under all of the socks and shirts that she probably sensed smelled like me. All of this led to more clothes cleaning and repacking. Then when I set the suitcase next to my bedroom door, ready to go, one of the cats sprayed the outside of the suitcase. It was a cloth bag; and I found it nearly impossible to clean it so that it no longer smelled of cat urine. I ended up spraying it with a lot of deodorant spray. That wasn't much better, really.

Of course, the day before the big trip is when anything that can go wrong will go wrong. If it wasn't something at work screaming for my attention to stay, then it was something at home demanding my full attention.

Peaches, on this occasion, had an accident. The former stray had blossomed with a better diet into a beautiful orange and white cat that looked pretty healthy. His weight had improved; and he showed no health problems as a result of his months of roughing it outdoors on his own. He had adjusted well to the house and spent at least half of his day indoors now. He had even taken to jumping up on window sills to sleep, with a great view of the outside world below our upper duplex.

That's proved to be his downfall. The kitchen window, propped wide open with a stick to hold it up, collapsed down upon him one fateful night. Without making a sound, he curled into bed with me and lay still. I began to pet him and immediately noticed that he was bleeding badly from his mouth.

I ran to the bathroom for towels and hydrogen peroxide to clean the cuts. He lay limp in bed until I returned.

I cleaned up the outside of his mouth and then pried open his jaw to see the internal damage. It was extensive. He had some mangled teeth. This puzzled me until I got up the next morning to take him to the vet and discovered that our kitchen window had collapsed on him. The stick that I used to prop the window open hadn't broken that I could see, but had apparently become dislodged, allowing the heavy window to fall upon him. The poor thing was probably napping when it crushed his jaw.

I had just about enough time to rush him to the vet for emergency dental surgery. He lost a number of teeth but would be alright. Of course, he had to take oral medication for several days after the dental surgery.

That meant more work for Deb in my absence.

110

"Don't worry about a thing," she told me when I brought Peaches home from the vet. My roll-on luggage for the trip was already by the door when I deposited Peaches in her arms. He was still woozy from his operation. The doctor had him pretty well sedated for the extensive oral surgery.

"I hope you will have the time to go through all of this follow-up medication," I said, holding up the little white bag of drugs the veterinarian had given me. "I'm sorry to put all of this on your shoulders. Is that alright? I could try to find a neighbor or someone at work to help, if it's too much."

She just smiled.

"Don't worry about it," she repeated. "Peaches and I are old friends. I am happy to spend the time with him. And he'll be no trouble. He understands that he needs help and trusts me completely. Medicating him will be super easy."

Droopy eyes on Peaches told me that he wasn't scared or concerned. He just clung to her, as she held him gently in her arms. His eyes fluttered open and shut. He was at peace.

"How about your cold?" I suddenly remembered. "Did you have a chance to get anything for your cold; or do you want me to run to the drug store for you?"

She just smiled.

"Got it all covered," she said. "Now don't worry. You'd better get going, or you're going to miss your flight."

I grabbed my roll-on suitcase and slid past Deb and the cat in her arms to make my exit. Actually, I had about five last-minute things to do at the office before I left. So, with my mind on my new cat and Deb, I tried to plow through the stack of papers on my desk, moving some things onto other desks to get rid of them and putting things needed for the trip into my case. I was certain to forget something. I always did. I just couldn't get my mind off Deb and the cat. I needed to be there at the house. Deb, on the other hand, needed to fly away somewhere. Why is life so twisted around?

Preoccupied with so many nagging concerns, I started to take the wrong road to the airport and nearly arrived late. I parked in the long-term lot at the Lindberg Terminal and took the shuttle to the gate. Canada today. England soon after my return.

I had to focus. I was supposed to visit our publisher's distributor in Montreal and present the new line of books that we were promoting for release next season. That meant a slide show. Did I have everything for the slide show? My heart stopped for a minute, as I sat waiting to board the plane. No time for mistakes now. Yes, I had the slides. But no projector. Had I asked them to set up a projector in Montreal? I thought so. It was so hard to focus. And then I started to worry whether the sales reps in Montreal would expect my presentation to be both in English and French, since it was a bilingual country and Quebec was primarily French. I had never presented to this Canadian distributor's sales reps before and did not know what to expect. My high school French was very weak at this point.

Get a grip on yourself, I told myself. Leave home behind you. Focus on the job, on the trip. That was all that mattered at the moment. Things at home would take care of themselves. It would all be there when I got back. It always worked that way.

Suddenly I wished that I had one of those communication devices that they used on Star Trek. Our publishing house had one cell phone, but it was a big, white brick that was so large and cumbersome to carry and use that nobody had much interest in it. I think the president's wife had it – the new gadget.

I walked onto the plane and rested my eyes. In no time at all, I found myself in Montreal at the distributor's seasonal gathering of sales reps. When I walked into the room, the sales manager from New World Library was wrapping up his presentation of their new line. And I was delighted to see that he was using a slide projector. I sat next to him and smiled, thinking that I might need to borrow the projector when he finished, if it belonged to him.

He spoke only in English and finished quickly. He answered a last question from the group and sat down. Then he and I started to chat. I asked him about the projector. He told me that the slide projector was not his own but had been supplied by the distributor. I got my Kodak carousel of slides out of the case and started to cue up my presentation to the first slide and the first book that I would present.

The light went on after New World Library's sales manager stood up to leave. I stood up to introduce myself and begin my presentation.

"Hi, I said. "I bring you greetings from Minnesota. I have some wonderful slides of our great new book covers to show you, if my cats didn't pee on them."

That got a good laugh. I was actually serious.

I sailed through all of the books that we were releasing in the months ahead. In the end, there were no questions - only applause. That was fine with me, only because it meant I was finished early and could go home.

In no time at all, I found myself on the return flight to America's heartland. Now that the Montreal trip was behind me, I started to obsess again about the cats and Peaches in particular. Deb certainly had her hands full this time. I wondered whether there was any way I could make it up to her. I had not bought any gift for her in Canada, since my trip was so short. And soon I would be flying off to England for another sales presentation on the new line of books. It was dizzying.

After the flight, I rushed up the stairs to our second-floor duplex at the old Victorian house. Everything was calm. There were no cat odors. The place was clean. Cats came out to greet me. Deb wasn't home yet. But I could see that Peaches was doing well and looked fine. He stood on one end of the sofa and let me pick him up. I stroked him about the ears and then the around the jaws. He didn't seem to wince. What an amazing recovery, I thought. I wished that people could recover that easily from physical pain and trauma. There were no indications, I could detect, that he was even emotionally upset.

I was upstairs emptying my suitcase and putting things away in my bedroom when I heard Deb come home. She often schlepped big bags with her and always dropped her heavy purse with a thud when she got upstairs to the living room at the top of the front stairs.

Before I could ask her how things had gone with the cats and everything, she started asking about my trip. I told her I wanted to bring her home a souvenir or something but didn't have a chance. Time was short.

She waved this off.

"We had a great time here while you were gone!" she said. "Peachy-boy took his medicine like a big

115

boy and he's doing just fine now. I don't think he had any pain with the medication. He was in good spirits. He just wanted to be held and cuddled. He's a real cuddle kitty. He loves it here. I think he's in heaven just to have a home and people who care for him."

I told her that was great and thanked her.

"Who wouldn't want to live in our home?" she added. "It's like a Victorian castle. My friends can't believe how cool it is."

Deb started upstairs but slipped on the first few steps.

"You sorta got ahead of yourself there," I teased. "Remember - one step at a time."

She stopped for a moment.

"You know, I just can't shake this cold," she said. "I've had it for about a week now."

I told her that a week wasn't long for a cold and that mine sometimes hung around for a month or so.

"Oh, I'll be fine long before a month is up," Deb said. "It just bugs me. It's getting hard to concentrate at work, with my head pounding. I feel all congested upstairs."

I suggested some liquid cold medicine for congestion associated with colds and reminded her that we had a bottle of it on the window ledge by the kitchen sink. She waved that notion away with one hand, as though she had things totally under control.

Well, Wizard always had her back. With him, she had beaten the odds, pushing back terminal cancer as few others had done. She ate a healthy diet, got plenty of sleep, had little stress that I could see, and didn't smoke. I envied Deb Bennett.

"You know," she told me, sitting at our big kitchen table, "I always said that I would never go out with anyone who smoked. Date anyone like that, I mean. Well, I have found an exception."

It was good to hear her repeat that she was still happy with her new boyfriend. She needed some fun in her life and some new friends. So, I listened with interest as she sang his praises once again.

"This new guy I met," Deb beamed, "is younger than me. He lives here in the area and is a lot of fun. We've done a few things together; and I think I like him. He's funny and sensitive. A sweet guy. Young, but mature. So, it's good for now, I mean... We'll see. I'm taking things slow. I'm just enjoying the moment, enjoying the company."

I turned my head to look at her more directly before responding.

"You deserve some fun, some happy moments for all you've gone through," I said. "All work and sleep, just hanging out at home isn't enough. Get out and live a little. You've earned that."

She just smiled. We sat there quiet for a moment, as the words sank in.

Then she abruptly sprang to her feet and moved toward the kitchen sink. She reached into the overhead counter near the sink and removed her Proctor-Silex coffee grinder. She swiveled around with the grinder in one hand and set it down on the peninsula counter, with me on the other side of the counter. She plugged in the grinder and then turned around again to retrieve a bag of whole coffee beans from the refrigerator.

She poured beans from the bag into the coffee grinder, without measuring. She fit the lid over the grinder and pressed the button on the Proctor-Silex. The beans swirled around with a lot of noise. She seemed to know exactly how long to grind the beans. When she removed the lid to examine her finely ground coffee, she looked across the counter at me, still seated at the table.

"Umm!" she said. "A perfect coffee. Sound good?"

I nodded, smelling the rich aroma of the fresh coffee released from the grinder.

She reached across the counter for her French coffee press and poured the ground beans into the press.

At the kitchen sink, she filled the press with water and set it on the counter to brew.

"You can use this coffee grinder and my French press any time you want," she told me, watching the coffee beginning to darken the water. "Just no flavored beans, okay? Don't put any flavored coffee beans in the grinder. No vanilla-flavored beans, no hazel nut beans, or cinnamon. Just real coffee. How can you improve on coffee, right? It's perfect."

I promised not to foul her grinder with strange flavors that didn't belong there, which seemed to please her.

Looking around the kitchen, I could fully appreciate how she had made herself at home there. Her coffee maker, her clock on the wall, her microwave. She had made it homey; and it felt better with her there.

The next day, I went over the feeding of the cats and care of the plants. It was more of a courtesy to make certain that she was comfortable caring for my part of the house. It was also my way of preparing things neatly for her, instead of simply skipping out again and dumping everything on her. She already knew how to care for the cats and plants better than I could, of course. I had no doubt about that. And, frankly, it felt safe to have her there in charge.

I rolled out the front door with my little roll-on suitcase and looked back quickly to see if the cats were putting up a fuss at my leaving. One of my cats was sitting on Deb's lap, fully engrossed in her petting.

"Go!" she told me. "Everything will be fine here."

I did not call Deb during my short trip, which ran across me like a blur of airports, hotels, and handshakes. My new Canadian trip – short sales presentations to buyers at book chains Smithbooks and Cole's, was over in no time. In two days, I found myself walking routinely through our front door, as though I'd never left. It seemed like a revolving door; and my head was spinning from the travel as I returned to our house.

As soon as I retrieved my keys from the front door, I glanced around to see whether anything had changed. Everything was neat and clean. The plants looked healthier. Some of the cats were lounging on the living room sofa, with others sleeping on the faded, green carpet. None of them seemed anxious to see me, as I returned. Everything was tranquil.

Deb sat rocking in her wicker chair close to the television set, which held her attention fast. Wizard was on her lap. Peaches was sitting faithfully next to her.

I shouted a greeting, and finally she looked up from the television. She was absorbed again in a classic episode of Star-Trek. Wherever it appeared on the dial, she could find it

She rose from the rocker and struggled to hold her balance. Rockers are not the most stable chairs, and her sudden enthusiasm caught the chair moving one way, while she was moving another direction.

"I think we need to cut you off at the bar, young lady!" I teased, knowing full well that her healthy life style did not include imbibing.

"Too much caffeine," she countered. "It got me jumpy, I guess."

She was still wearing one of her red Lancôme blazers from the cosmetic counter. Usually, she raced upstairs to her bedroom as soon as she got home from work to hang up her coat from work. I figured that she had gotten home a little later and plopped down immediately to relax before changing.

She put one hand on the front of her red blazer, self-consciously.

"Long day," she said. "I'm really tired. How was your trip? Cats are all fine. They missed you, of course."

I shrugged off the question about the trip. It was just work, not a fun trip. Of course, to Deb who had never really traveled, a plane trip to Canada probably sounded like fun and adventure.

"I see that the cats are all sleeping, happy as little clams," I said. "You must have them charmed.

121

Thanks a bunch. Hope they weren't too much trouble."

She shook her head sideways.

"Hey, she said, "I want to show you something in the back yard. Is now a good time, or do you want to unpack and rest first?"

"No," I said. "So, what's up?"

"Oh, nothing's wrong or anything," she said. "I just wanted to show you an idea I have for the backyard, if it's okay with you."

We walked down the back stairs near the kitchen to take us into the back yard. It was a steep, long staircase and no doubt unfamiliar to her. Deb led the way. She clutched the hand rail and went down very slowly, one step at a time. Most people went into the backyard through the side gate outside and didn't take the stairs. It was dark on the back staircase.

When we reached the bottom, I helped her open the back door, which had a big, sliding bolt lock in addition to the lock on the doorknob. That door opened to a little pass-through room with shelves and clutter that I really should have organized by now. I flicked on the light for this little room and then opened the outer storm door that lead to the back yard.

It was still light enough outside to see the yard fairly well. The back yard hadn't been landscaped but was a large grassy area with a fence all around it.

Without advancing beyond the door, Deb pointed to the far corner of the yard, where the grass gave way to a muddy uphill slope.

"I was thinking about a burn pit that we could put back there. We could make it out of stones or bricks, maybe. Anyway, we were back here yesterday – this guy and me, sitting in the back yard. We thought how much fun it would be to sit around a big fire pit."

I knew that she loved the outdoors from her descriptions of We Fest. She would take her sleeping bag on these summer outings. Campfires were a part of it.

"Sure," I said. "Not much summer left, but maybe I could get some curved blocks and put something together by next spring," I said. "I have one last summer trip to London coming up. Then the Frankfurt International book fair in the fall. But we can begin planning it. Yes, we could make it really fun back her with a big fire pit. And we could make it with seating all around it, too. Why not."

She nodded up and down happily and then turned to go up the stairs.

I thought about getting the blocks and mortar for the fire pit before I left for London, but soon found myself swamped at work, just trying to catch up from the last trip and needing to get ready to be gone on the next one. I'd be gone a little longer this trip, but then I'd be through with most of my travel, with just one more trip in the fall. Then we could focus on making our home comfortable. I looked forward to that.

In another week or so, I found myself walking out the front door again, with my roll-on suitcase fully stuffed and another shoulder bag packed with necessary business materials for the London trip.

As before, I was on a mission for the publishing company. I had to present the new line of books that we planned for release in the coming season. I had slides of the book covers and physical prints of the book covers, along with descriptions of the new releases. This trip was for the sales representatives of the European book distributors, primarily covering the UK excluding half of old Ireland. I also tried to visit some of the leading book stores in London during these trips.

Sometimes I stayed in a haunted guest house in London, a row house converted to rooms with shared baths on each tiny floor. That place on Avonmore Street was close to the London book fair exhibition hall in the spring. This trip, a little later in the year, took me on a train north of London where the wholesale distributor held its seasonal presentations in the meeting room of a resort hotel. So my lodging was not in South Kensington, but closer to the train station. I would have preferred staying at the resort hotel, but it must have been expensive to rent a room there. The grounds were beautifully maintained with carefully manicured shrubbery and clumps of brilliant flowers everywhere. And the meeting room was catered with lovely tea and treats, of course. Someday, I vowed, my Victorian house in Saint Paul might resemble this place, if only I could slow down the merry-go-round and get things organized properly.

Once again, the presentations went well. The slide show always went well. It was simple entertainment. Admittedly, though, I was jet-lagged during my oral presentation, talking over the slides. But the art carried the day. I needed to get home and become a home body.

When I finally got home, I found Deb in sort of a blue mood. She was sitting in the kitchen with the TV off and lights turned down. The cats were somewhere else.

I asked her whether anything was wrong, or if she was just tired from work. She'd been working late hours.

"Long days lately," she said in a low voice. "I'm a little bit drained. But I'm okay. I'm just tired."

I asked her whether things at work were alright.

"I'm pretty much all alone there," she said of the Dayton's cosmetics counter at the Roseville Mall.

"I'm supposed to have some help – one other person at least."

"No help?" I asked.

She went back into her usual complaint about work.

"Well, I have someone else in our department, but she's off in the back most of the time. She's off wearing the white lab coat. I'd like to get into that end of things, too. I mean, I've been there longer than her. A lot longer. They probably even pay her more. They are giving her more opportunities. I'm stuck all day behind the counter. I can't even go to the bathroom when I need to, or there would be nobody at the counter.

"I have to make all the signs, figure out the sale prices for markdowns, set things out on display, keep track of sales, and still handle all of the customers and people who have questions or might want a sample makeover. It's too much. Sometimes I feel stressed out."

I sympathized. And I noticed once again that she was still wearing her red Lacombe Paris blazer from work. She hadn't even changed from work, which is what she usually did as soon as she reached home. I guess she had to keep that red blazer clean and pressed to wear every day.

I offered to make her tea. She answered that she'd had a lot of coffee and was buzzing.

Deb rose slowly from the table and worked her way to the stairs leading upstairs to her bedroom. Maybe listening to her stereo in her room would help, I thought. She liked music in her room.

She stumbled on the second step and grabbed the hand rail.

"Watch that first step!" I called out.

She said nothing but continued slowly up the stairs.

The next morning, she told me that her nagging cold was wearing her down; and she apologized for sounding a little irritable the night before.

She was out the door to work before I left the house. The red blazer was back in play.

Chapter 6
Late *September 1992*

The grueling international book fair in Frankfurt, Germany later that fall left me drained upon my return. It's the longest book fair that anyone attends, and it runs for eight long days. Everybody in book publishing from around the world tries to attend if possible; and thousands and thousands of people speaking every language under the sun cram into the three large buildings that hold the many distributors. Most people don't make it "around the world," in the sense of seeing every exhibit down every aisle in all three buildings. They are too busy with scheduled appointments. That is particularly true of exhibitors, such as our niche publishing house. Two people usually attended from our publishing house; and still we were stuck most of every day with appointments scheduled weeks in advance. It is essentially a literary rights fair where translation rights are negotiated, and sample books distributed for consideration. And all of that is exhausting, particularly for the exhibitors.

Of course, it's also fun to visit Germany, eat foreign food every day, stay in quaint German hotels, ride buses to the fair, stroll the streets at night, and meet interesting people from around the world. Some people even give you little presents, if you have established a friendly rapport over time.

I'm certain that Deb expected exciting stories about living and playing in Germany for two weeks when I finally made in through our front door back in Minnesota. It would be the trip of a lifetime for her. To me it mostly represented eight long days of negotiations in a publisher's booth plus long plane rides that left my ears plugged.

Where were the fancy European chocolates that I had found for her? I boarded the plane in Germany with two beautiful boxes of fine chocolates, tied with gold ribbons. But I was so tired upon arrival in Minnesota that I forgot to reach up behind my jam-packed little suitcase in the overhead storage compartment to retrieve them. All I was thinking about at that point was grabbing my suitcase and returning home to sleep.

I did call the airline, but naturally the exotic boxes of chocolates had not been turned in as lost items when staff cleaned the airplane. They were treasures not easily found on this side of the Atlantic Ocean.

The boxes of chocolates were meant to be gifts for Deb for all of the work that she did gratis during my long absence. I also felt a little guilty for taking all of these glamorous, foreign trips, while she'd never been able to travel.

She would have loved Germany. My work partner and I were walking along the river Rhine one night where we found a huge tent with a circus show. It turned out to be none other than the famous Cirque de Solei.

In preparation for this German trip, I had learned enough words and common phrases to say thanks and good morning without much of an accent. I even learned enough German in the short time that I visited to walk into a restaurant on my own and order dinner without a hitch. My colleague on this trip was our foreign rights sales manager Margit Ifkowitch, who had left Germany as a girl and still led a German-American group in Minnesota that encouraged people to speak German. It helped to have her correct my German before venturing out on my own.

One thing Deb would not have liked about my dream trip to Germany, I'm certain, is the amount of smoking at the Frankfurt International Book Fair. I was one of the worst offenders, as I smoked my pipe at our booth all day long. Nobody seemed to care, or at least nobody complained about smoking in public back then. Not in Germany, at least.

I decided to stop smoking my pipe in our house when I returned home, because I knew that Deb didn't like smoking. She lived a healthy life. Besides, her nagging cold seemed to still have hold of her. I figured that second-hand smoke was the last thing she needed.

It's odd that I didn't think of that earlier. A smoke-filled room contributed nothing to the ambiance of our home. The windows were always dirty. You could scarcely see the TV through the smoke. Back then, it was acceptable to smoke in front of others. But, obviously, it was unthoughtful and unhealthy. It made breathing difficult, especially if you were already congested.

One of the first things that Deb told me when I got back was that her cold was still hanging on. Somehow, I didn't think that terribly odd, because I have often had summer colds that lasted for several weeks. I immediately asked whether she had anything to treat the cold. She said that she just needed more sleep.

I announced that I would not smoke in the house when she told me her nagging cold still bothered her. She felt dizzy, she said, and all clogged up. That's the same way summer colds would bother me, too - headaches and congestion.

I asked whether she'd had any of her girlfriends over to visit. She said not. She was going into work every day and just coming home to lie low. I hate nagging colds, so I could really empathize.

My first night back, we spoke very little. She retired to bed early and slowly walked up the stairs to her bedroom on the top floor. She did look weary.

 I noticed that she tripped on one of the first stairs again.

"Watch that first step!" I warned her again.

She turned her head slowly to give me sort of a dirty look. That wasn't like Deb. I figured she was really under the weather and very tired.

"Sorry," I added. "Bad joke. You okay?"

"Just this cold," she said. "I'll be better in a few days. I just need lots of rest."

Sleeping just down the hallway, I expected to hear her cough, sneeze, or get up a lot during the night. But apparently, she just slept like a log. All of my cats piled into my room and jockeyed for positions on my little bed. Seemingly, they didn't want to be around her cold. I know my cats didn't like to be around me whenever I coughed or sneezed. I'd had allergies during the summer, but they were long gone now that it was fall.

The next morning, I asked Deb if she wanted to help me to collect some blocks for the fire pit she had asked me to construct in back of our house. She just gave me a blank look, as though the concept didn't really register. Well, I'm sure that it was the last thing on her mind.

I asked her whether she'd had any interesting dates with her young boyfriend – the one who smoked. But she had not gone out anywhere in the past two weeks.

Well, lie low, I thought. Plenty of rest and down time out of the weather probably would be the best things for her.

I showed her some books that I had gathered on the trip. I told her about the fancy boxes of chocolates that I had brought on the plane for her and apologized for forgetting about them in the overhead when we landed.

She just shrugged it off without much enthusiasm.

I wondered whether she had lost interest in our relationship or living at the house or if she just felt under the weather and naturally depressed. I didn't know how to help her and didn't even know whether I could.

The coffee wasn't as good that morning, because I made it with my old can of commercial ground stuff in my drip pot. Not that Deb drank much of it.

When I left for work, she was still sitting at the kitchen table in her comfortable lounging clothes.

"No work today, then?" I asked on my way out.

"I think I need a down day," she said. "I need to take it easy until I'm feeling a little better."

"They'll miss you," I offered.

"Right," she said. "They'll really miss me."

When I got home, she was in her bedroom. I knocked on the door and asked if I could bring her any dinner. She said she'd be down in a few minutes to get something herself. I heard no music or TV coming from her room.

I made enough dinner for two, and eventually she did come downstairs to our kitchen. She gratefully accepted a bowl of soup but ate very little of it.

When she left the table to return to her room, she approached the stairway carefully, clutching the rail dearly. She stumbled again on the second step.

I moved closer to her.

"Are you sure you're okay?" I asked her.

"Just this nagging cold," she said again. "I'm so congested, I can hardly think straight."

"Have you been to see a doctor?"

"No big thing," she said. "I'll be okay."

I watched her slowly ascend the stairs, one step at a time. Then I sat down in the living room to think things over. Deb never missed work. She was always upbeat.

The phone rang, breaking my concentration.

I returned to the kitchen, where the wall-mount house phone was located.

134

On the other end of the phone, a woman named Sandra asked me if I was Deb's landlord. I answered yes.

"I work with Deb at Dayton's," she said. "I'm worried about her. She didn't come in today and didn't tell anyone that she was not coming. That's not like her."

"Yes, she said she has a bad cold," I said. "She's had it for some time now."

"Well, there are other things, too," Sandra said. "She's had a hard time at work lately. She had to prepare a lot of sale signs and markdowns, and she did it okay. But it took her a long time, and I could tell that she was having a hard time concentrating."

"Wow," I said.

"Yeah, wow," she said. "That's not like Deb. And I'm wondering if she's been to see a doctor."

"I asked her that today. She said no, that it's just a cold."

There was a long pause from Sandra.

"You know about her medical history, right?" she asked me.

I answered yes, but admitted that I hadn't known Deb very long.

"Well, that's what worries me," Sandra said of her medical history. "She had a brain tumor. They shrank it. Now she has trouble with her balance."

"She trips every time she walks up the stairs to her room," I said.

"That's what I mean. See? Maybe I'm over-reacting. I hope so. I know that she goes into a clinic regularly to be checked out. They would have found something if the cancer had returned, right? They would have told her. She'd know."

"She hasn't mentioned anything about that," I said. "She insists that she just has a bad cold."

"Does it seem like a cold to you?"

"I see what you mean," I said. "She doesn't cough or sneeze. Wow… Wow…. What should we do?"

"I dunno," Sandra said. "But I think we should do something. And soon. They don't pay her for days off without some sort of medical reason. She might lose her job. I'd hate to see that."

"She's been there a long time," I said.

"Years," Sandra said.

"Does she have decent medical coverage from work?" I asked. "What does it cover?"

Sandra said she'd check tomorrow and get right back to me. She said she wanted to take charge of the situation immediately.

I volunteered to help in any way I could.

"That's good," she said. "We might need a lot of help to pull this off."

The next day, I was anxious for Sandra's call. I worried that if I didn't hear from her that I would have trouble finding her. I had Deb's parents and work number on her rental application but did not have Sandra's contact information.

But Sandra did call me as soon as I got home the next day. She asked if Deb could be listening.

I told her that we had a house phone with extensions throughout the house, but that Deb was not downstairs and probably wasn't listening. Her room upstairs was quiet; so I assumed that she was sleeping again.

"Well, I went to HR today with another one of Deb's friends here at work - Anita," Sandra said. "I went over Deb's situation and what her options might be. It's not good that she didn't call it sick, but just failed to show up. But I explained that she's probably too sick to call in."

I told her that Deb's last rent check had bounced. She promptly gave me a new one, a check that she neatly stuck to the wall near my bedroom door with a safety pin. Unfortunately, that check bounced too. Deb was out of funds. I began to wonder to myself just how many days of work Deb had missed recently.

"She can't miss work," Sandra said. "HR said they'd pay for any sort of medical exam that she might need. She has pretty much full medical coverage, but they will need everything documented."

I let it all sink in for a moment before asking the big question that was eating at me.

"I'm not sure at all that Deb will go for a medical exam," I said. "I don't know if we can get her to a doctor. She's sort of in a state of denial."

"I know," Sandra said. "Any ideas?"

"Well, you probably know her better than I do," I said. "She's only lived here a few months."

"But she respects you," Sandra said. "She talks about you. And she doesn't exactly trust me lately."

I asked her for an explanation.

"Oh, just stupid work stuff," Sandra said. "Nothing, really. But let's just say that I'm not her favorite person just now."

"You're the one with the white lab coat?" I asked.

"Bingo," she said.

"I'm just worried that – I hate to bring it up, but I'm just worried that Deb's cancer might have returned. She said it was totally cleared up and that she was in full remission."

"I know," Sandra said. "That's what she told me, too."

"That would be the worst," I said, "but it would explain a lot."

"Uh, huh."

"So, what's the game plan?" I asked. "What do you want me to do. Just tell me."

"Well," Sandra said, "I think we need an intervention. We need to get as many people together as we can – people that Deb might listen to. We need to convince her to get a full medical exam."

"When?" I asked.

"Soon," she said. "Very soon. Like tomorrow. Today would be better."

"Set it up," I said. "I don't know any of her people, only you. I've never met any of them."

Sandra promised to call me back as soon as she could. She told me to stay close to the phone and keep my schedule open. She wanted to hold the intervention there at the Dayton house. I suggested that we do it in the evening. She said that it would almost have to be in the evening for most people to attend.

True to her word, Deb's friend called me back within an hour or two. She said we'd get together the very next night at my house and to make sure

Deb was home. She didn't want me to tell her about the meeting until people had arrived.

I figured that keeping Deb at home would be the least of our problems. She was now spending almost all of her time sleeping in her bedroom.

But when I came home that next night, Deb was not at home. I stated to panic. I saw that her little, red car was gone, but had no way of knowing where she might be.

Fortunately, she returned soon before anyone else had arrived. She was carrying a little, white bag from Bobar Drug Store near our house. She set it on a chair in the kitchen area.

"I lost Willow," she said, hanging her head in despair. "I didn't know she followed me out to the car. Before I knew it, she had jumped in the car. But then I figured she'd be okay riding with me. I only went to the drug store up on Grand Avenue. Bobar's. But after I went to the store, I open the car door and she jumped out. I tried to catch her, but she ran across Grand Avenue. Cars blocked me from following her. After the traffic cleared, I couldn't see her anywhere. I called for her and looked. But I have no idea where she might have gone."

I told her that I would make a nice color flier and put copies everywhere near the spot where she lost him. I told her not to worry, that she wasn't feeling up to looking any more just now.

Then the doorbell rang, and the first of many people invited to Deb's intervention sat down with us in the living room. I told Deb that I'd asked some of her friends over to visit with her, since she hadn't been to work and was feeling poorly. She was too weary to put much thought into what I was telling her. She just sat there, surrounded by friends. We formed a semi-circle, sitting on the two sofas and chairs in the living room. Deb sat in her wicker rocker that was now turned away from the TV and part of the semi-circle of chairs. I sat next to her, just to make certain that she stayed put and stayed calm. Naturally, she was a little wary about what was taking place, being the focus of so much sudden attention.

"Deb," I began, "your friends were worried about you when you didn't come to work. They are concerned that you are sick. So, I invited some of them over to the house to pay you a visit and offer you some support."

She gave me a puzzled look.

"And I offered to contact some of your friends from work and coordinate a home visit," Sandra quickly interjected. "Only because we care for you. We wanted to make sure that you are okay."

Deb turned abruptly to face Sandra on the other side of her.

"I lost my cat Willow tonight," Deb said. "Will you help me find her? I went to Bobar Drug Store up on Grand. Willow slipped out of the house and into the car. When I got to Bobar's and opened the door, she jumped out. She can't be too far. She never goes outside, so she's probably hiding somewhere near Bobar Drugs."

"We'll look for Willow," I told her. "Don't worry. I will put up fliers and go door to door all around the area."

"Yes," Sandra said. "Let's focus now on how you feel. Have you been to a doctor?"

"Oh, I go to a clinic regularly for check-ups," Deb said. "I've done that ever since my recovery, since remission. I've been careful to watch my health."

"So, what do you think is wrong?" Anita asked.

"Just a bad cold," Deb said. "I just can't shake it. I feel tired all the time, like I'm living in a fog. I'm really congested."

"But you haven't been to see a doctor about it?" Sandra challenged her. "Recently, I mean."

"No need," Deb said. "I know it's just a bad cold. I got some medicine for it."

"At Bobar Drug?" I asked.

"I told you I was fine," she answered.

"Well, I checked with HR," Sandra said. "We don't want you to lose any paid days. If you document that you are sick, you could qualify for sick leave.

But you need to see a doctor. HR said you're covered to go somewhere to get checked out by whoever you need to see. And maybe they could get you back on your feet and feeling better soon."

"Uh, huh," Deb said. "I'll look into that."

"Let's do it first thing," Sandra said. "I'll come by tomorrow and take you to a doctor myself. I'll take you to Fairview South Medical Center. They'll give you a full exam."

"I don't need a hospital. Fairview is a hospital."

"Well, they're the best and will give you a thorough exam," Sandra said. "I'll even drive you there and stay with you while you're there. Tomorrow morning, okay? I'll come get you at 9 am, okay?"

"But you can't miss work," Deb countered.

"Don't worry about me," Sandra assured her. "HR cleared it. They think it's a great idea to take you in for some tests."

"Okay," Deb said. "I'll be ready."

Sandra turned to me.

"And you watch her carefully tonight, okay?" Sandra told me. "Make sure she's ready when I get here tomorrow at 9. Make her coffee – breakfast, if she'll eat it."

I nodded.

Looking around the room, I wondered how many of these people were close friends and how many were simply co-workers. There were no family members. I might have called her parents, since I did have their phone number from Deb's rental application form. But this was the group Sandra had brought together with very little notice and very little debate. Only a few of us had spoken. The rest were more like witnesses. But it did create a more formidable presentation. Deb put up very little opposition. But she hadn't been eager to go back into a hospital. She'd had too much of that in the past and obviously wanted to avoid them. Sandra's offer to escort her there first thing in the morning with company backing seemed like a solid plan.

When Sandra arrived a little early the next morning, I told them both that I couldn't go, because I needed to hang up fliers for Deb's lost cat before going to work. I promised to stay involved and urged Sandra to call me if needed.

Deb took only her purse and a light coat. Missing was Deb's hat, Deb's signature look. I guess she didn't think that a trip to the hospital for an exam was that big of an ordeal.

Once I saw Sandra help her friend into the car and drive away from the house, I grabbed the fliers for Willow and my staple gun. Soon I was back at work, wishing that I had given Sandra my work number. Well, she probably knew where I worked. But I figured that no news on that day was probably good news.

As soon as I got home after work that day, the phone rang.

Chapter 7
October-November 1992

Sandra called me from the hospital in Edina. She said that she had checked Deb into Fairview South for a complete medical exam and had gone over her medical history, as best she could outline it. Sandra's voice sounded stilted and distant, as though she were not totally present.

"Listen, now," she said. "Deb has gone through some simple tests and has been seen by a team of doctors here. But they haven't released her. She is resting in a bed; and they would like to prep her for more tests tomorrow."

I hesitated to ask her anything more.

"Do they think the cancer might have returned?"

"Well, they are definitely concerned about that. They have looked into her medical history and contacted her parents. They don't want to waste any time getting to the bottom of things. Just in case, you know...."

"What's next?" I asked. "Are we out of the picture now, with her parents on board?"

"No, not exactly," Sandra said. "They want us all there to go over the situation, just as soon as they know more. Can you make it? They want to go over everything with us, in case they find something major. They want our input."

"But maybe it's nothing," I argued. "When will they know for certain?"

"Look," Sandra said. "Just come as soon as you can. Deb will need friends around her. Maybe the doctors will know something by the time you get here. Let's hope for the best. Maybe they'll even send her home soon. I dunno."

"But they think the cancer's back," I said again. "They think she has a brain tumor. I knew it. That's why she's been walking around in a fog, tripping on the stairs and getting dizzy when she stands up too fast."

"We'll see," Sandra said. In the meantime, we can hope for the best, right?"

I didn't know what to say.

"So, you're coming tonight, right?" Sandra said. "Deb will want reassuring faces around her bed. It's a pretty scary situation for her."

Sandra gave me the floor and room number for the meeting room at the hospital. It was on the same floor where Deb was waiting in a bed.

"But you should come here tonight to see Deb," she insisted. "She's pretty concerned. She knows what might be at stake; and she knows how tough this can be for her. She would like to see you; and she can have visitors.

Sandra gave me the location again and the best hours to visit. In a case like Deb's, they seem pretty lenient at the hospital here. She was not in recovery, but in a bed in the cancer ward, going through tests and evaluation.

In the interest of saving time to get up to see Deb before she went to sleep, I skipped dinner and dashed to the copy center to make more copies of my lost cat flier. Fortunately, the copy center was near my home and didn't take me much out of my way. Unfortunately, the flier was a hand-made plea to call or return the missing cat Willow to our address. "Long, gray fur, friendly but shy. Himalayan adult cat. No ID tags or collar. Our indoor cat got loose."

I slapped some more fliers onto street posts and telephone poles. I didn't have time to do anything more. I needed to get to the hospital fast. They would probably give Deb some sleeping pills or something to give her a good night's sleep before further poking and probing. I could only imagine how intrusive and frightening that would be to a young woman who had gone through years of brain cancer with a death sentence, only to find her miraculous remission had reversed itself. It would not be a relaxing night for her, preparing for final sentencing.

After a couple of wrong turns in the large hospital labyrinth, I found Deb in a small, side room in the cancer ward. There were no other patients stationed there. Deb was in a small bed, wrapped up pretty tightly. Her long, blond hair spilled onto both sides of the pillow; and I wondered how long she might keep those golden locks. Soon, they would be taking pictures of her head to determine whether the cancer had returned, if they hadn't already done so. On the other hand, she might be back home in a day, with proper medication to fight a bad cold or whatever was vexing her. But I had my doubts.

Judging from her worried expression, so did Deb. Sandra and Anita were both at Deb's bed side when I reached her room; and I could tell that they were happy to have another companion to keep Deb's spirits up. It looked like a tall challenge for any friend, as Deb looked like she was somewhere lost and trying to find her way out.

"Ola, roomy!" I called out in my most cheerful voice. "I bring you greetings from the home front. Our Victorian house misses you."

She looked at me, turning her head only slightly. Her eyes glued onto me; and they screamed out with unspoken fear.

"Did you find Willow?" she asked me abruptly. "Is Willow okay?"

"Don't worry," I said. "I have put up a lot of fliers, and tomorrow I will go door to door. I will check with the pet shelters. Willow could not be far away. She's probably in somebody's house, charming strangers now. I'll find her. I promise."

149

"How is Wizard?" she asked. "Does he miss her?"

"He misses you. But he's okay. He's one solid, little guy, isn't he? He's got it all together."

"That cat saved my life," Deb said. "He's amazing. Maybe he can do it again."

"You'll be okay," I said. "Let's not worry until all of the tests are in and we have the full picture."

"I thought I was done with all of this," she said. "Now here I am again."

"Things might look better in the morning," I countered.

"Watch after things for me, okay" Deb said.

"Sure. You got it, kiddo."

"No, I mean it," she said. "Lock my room. Put my things away. Don't let anyone get in there and take anything. And don't let them take my car."

"Who?" I asked.

"My parents. Don't let them take the car. Hide the keys."

I saw her purse and picked it up.

"You have the keys with you?" I asked.

She said nothing. I felt awkward going through her purse, so I just peeked into it and tried to scan the many contents with my eyes, without grabbing anything.

"Ah!" I said. "I see your keys." "The car keys are here with your house keys. They'll be okay. Just keep this purse here beside you. Put them in a drawer or something. Why would they take your car?"

"My dad did help me get that car," Deb said. "But don't let him take it. I'm going back to our home. I'm going back to our Victorian house in Saint Paul."

"You bet," I assured her.

Sandra gave me a sharp look.

"Let's see what another day brings," I reminded her. "You're in good hands here, right?"

Sandra cleared her voice.

"They originally said they would want to see all of us tonight at eight," Sandra told me, "but there are more tests scheduled for tomorrow. They will prep her in the morning for a CAT scan. So we can gather around Deb tomorrow night after work, okay? And it will be 8pm. Eight tomorrow night. On this floor. You can be here right?" she asked me.

"Of course," I said. "That will give me a little time to get things straightened out with the cat."

"They're going to give me a CAT scan," Deb said - "a CAT scan of my head."

I reminded her of our old joke about CAT scans and lab tests. I wondered if that was in poor taste.

"They will get a cat to jump up on your bed and scan you; and then if you need a second opinion, they will bring in a black Lab for a lab test."

She smiled a little but did not laugh.

"Have Deb's parents come by?" I asked Sandra in a somewhat softer voice. "Will they be here tomorrow night for the meeting?"

"I know that they were notified and have spoken to the doctors here," Sandra said in a hushed tone. "They filled in the hospital staff about Deb's medical history. I don't know if they 've been up to visit her yet, though."

"Have your parents been by to visit with you?" she asked Deb, speaking louder.

"My parents – yes," Deb answered. "They know everything."

A nurse came by and asked us to leave, so that Deb could get some rest, noting that she had a big day ahead of her tomorrow.

On my way home, I thought I'd drive by Bobar Drugs and post fliers in area stores. Also, I could ask neighbors if they had seen Deb's missing cat.

It was a beautiful, sweet cat and surely was taken indoors by the first door she encountered.

But when I reached Saint Paul, I realized that many of the Grand Avenue stores were already closed and that it was probably too late to knock on neighbors' doors, too. So, I planned to do that as soon as possible. I would also need to check with animal control and the local Humane Society to see if anyone had found the cat and brought it to a shelter. It was too late for all of that tonight.

After work the next night, I made a quick sandwich and then took off for the stores up on Grand Avenue where Willow had escaped from Deb's car. I thought about going door-to-door at area houses, but then noticed that I needed to get a rush on. The 8 o'clock meeting at Fairview South loomed large; and I wanted to stop by the animal control shelter and Humane Society.

I sped up the road where both were located, conveniently near each other. The city animal control shelter was closed. I went into the Humane Society, but there was a long line and few volunteers, so I decided to skip that for now and head out to the hospital in Edina. Traffic could be a problem that time of day. Maybe I could call the next day instead of visiting.

The hospital parking lot was crowded, so I parked in a questionable corner and rushed up to the fourth floor for Deb's meeting.

Sandra met me at the entrance to the cancer ward. Anita was with her.

"Hurry!" she said. "Everyone else is here; and they want to start."

We took a few turns until we reached a conference room with the door closed. Sandra pushed the door open, and I could see that a small crowd had already gathered. A doctor was there with a middle-aged man and woman I had never met. I assumed that they were Deb's parents from Forest Lake. It was about a 50-60-minute drive for them to reach this south Minneapolis suburb. Nobody else was there. The conference table was big enough for several more people.

"Isn't Deb included in our meeting?" I asked the doctor. She was a woman in her mid-thirties with dark hair, trim figure, and short height. She had a pen and writing pad with her. She also had medical files or reports folded on the table beside her.

"Not in this meeting," she told me. "This is for family – and, of course, Deb's other close relations. We are here to talk about Deb and what's best for her at this point."

"What did you find out?" I asked the doctor.

"As I've already told Debra's mother and father here," the lady doctor said, "the CAT scan told us that the cancer has returned, and that the tumor

154

appears to be spreading rapidly. So, we know that time is against us here. We took her immediately into surgery. I was one of the surgeons who worked on Debra. The cancer has spread extensively. We tried to get as much of it as we could, but we couldn't get it all."

I looked nervously around the room. Deb's parents just stood quietly with their heads down.

"This has been going on a long time," the doctor continued. "It's really advanced and apparently growing at a fast rate.

"I did check with the clinic where Deb has been going for follow-up tests. But the last time she went there, apparently, they did not do a CAT scan on Deb. I don't quite know why."

"What?" I questioned. "If they had done the CAT scan on her - done the proper thing, then the cancer would have been caught sooner, right?"

"Yes," the doctor said. "That's true."

"Well, would you testify to that effect?" I asked. "It sounds as though the clinic is negligent, right? Didn't they usually give her a CAT scan?"

"Yes, that would be normal procedure," the doctor said. "And I can't speak to what the clinic did or didn't do, and their reasons. But it is unfortunate that the return of the cancer was not detected any sooner. That's what the clinic was supposed to be monitoring."

"Would you be willing to say that in court?" I asked.

"Oh," the doctor faltered. "I don't know about that. I don't know all of the particulars and couldn't really address that."

"What lies ahead for Deb then?" Sandra asked. "She can't go back to work, can she?"

"No," the doctor said. "The cancer is too advanced for that. I'm surprised she has functioned as well as she has, really."

"Another operation?" I asked.

"We've done all that we can safely do as surgeons," the doctor said. "Now you have to explore your options - what is best for Deb. She's pretty sick. You'll need to make some decisions for her, I'm afraid."

"What are the options?" Sandra asked in a meek voice.

"It depends how aggressively you want to treat this," the doctor said. "You could do chemo-therapy. That might knock it out. It's painful, and not always successful, of course. But that's what we often can offer in these situations."

"Or?" Anita asked.

"Or, you could simply let nature take its course. You could put her in a restful place. Maybe she could go home, if you could arrange for enough people to care for her. She will need round-the-clock attention. That could be done with friends and family, if there are enough of you who are able to do that. Or else, you could find someplace for her. It's hard to get a bed. There's a waiting list."

Sandra looked around the room.

"I think it's just us," she said. "Anita and I work full-time. And Von works full time. I don't know about the two of you," she said, looking at Deb's parents.

Her parents said nothing.

"And I don't know who else we could get involved. It would be tough. But we could try."

"I'd be willing to help," I said. "But is that realistic? I mean, around the clock care?"

The doctor nodded her head.

"Yes, it's a lot harder than you might think and takes an awful lot. Don't feel badly if you can't do it. Most people can't."

"Well, what about chemotherapy then?" I asked. "I mean, that's something hospitals have a lot of experience doing in these cases, right? Maybe that would be successful. "

Everyone looked at the doctor.

"I mean, what are the odds?" I asked her. "Can you make some sort of educated guess?

"I can't give you odds, not really," she said. "But odds probably are against her at this stage. I wish I could say otherwise. But we need to face the truth."

The group was silent for a while.

"What would Deb want?" the doctor asked. "Has she given you any indication?"

I looked at Deb's parents.

"This is something we've been facing for a long time now," her mother said. "It's new to the rest of you, but we've been wrestling with this for years."

"I think Deb wants to live," I said. "She's only 32 years old. She's spent most of her adult life being sick and recovering from being sick. She's faced death before. Now she wants to live. We have to give her a chance, even if it's a small chance. Don't you think?"

Sandra muttered some sort of agreement that sounded like lukewarm support. Anita seemed to be nodding her head in agreement.

Her parents said nothing. Neither did the doctor.

"If that's what you all agree to do, then I can schedule her for treatments," the doctor said. "They can do that best at a hospital in Saint Paul.

158

Deb lives in Saint Paul. It's closer to her parents and where the rest of you live and work, right?"

Nobody said anything more.

The doctor started to gather up her papers. I noticed that she had brought a writing pad for notes but had written nothing on the pad. She took her time getting ready to leave, to allow any more discussion.

She stood up and slipped the files under one arm.

"Okay, then," she said. "I'll set it up and give you information as soon as I can as to when we will be moving her and where that's located."

She indicated that it might be a day before they moved Deb, as they wanted to observe her and monitor her post-surgery recovery period. I considered how odd the word recovery sounded in this context.

After the doctor had left the room, the rest of us sat there for an awkward moment or two. Then Deb's parents quietly walked out of the room, without engaging us. Then there were just Deb's three friends left around the table.

I wanted to scream. How could I have railroaded this decision? Why had they listened to me? I wanted to hide somewhere.

The three of us rose from our seats nervously and quietly filed out of the conference room and left the ward.

"If I hear something tomorrow, I will call you," Sandra told me. "The doctor has my number, but not yours.

I thanked her and wandered aimlessly toward my car, feeling dead inside.

Chapter 8
November 1992

Somehow, I felt optimistic about Deb, despite everything that we had discovered about her dire situation. The fall season lingered in the air, fighting off the dreary winter we all expected. For the moment, at least, autumn was alive with promise. The beautifully colored leaves were still mostly clinging to life on the many trees of Saint Paul. The sun was intense for that time of year. The freshness of the fall season seemed to offer hope that things would remain okay and that the cold death that people associate with winter was held in check. But autumn is a season of transition, so I knew that things would change. And winter doesn't really signal death, but only a time of retreat, with the promise of growth after the snow and cold.

I put up the last of the fliers for Deb's lost cat and knocked on a few neighborhood doors. I reasoned that somebody had found the beautiful Himalayan cat Willow to be irresistible and taken the charmer inside their home. Nobody was talking, whereas a beautiful stray cat on the street surely would have drawn attention and concern. I stopped worrying about Willow, whose owner was not at home to care for her, anyway. I focused fully on Deb and the series of hurdles that she would face very shortly in a life or death struggle to make it to spring.

Realizing that my next visit to Deb at the Fairview South cancer ward would probably be my last chance to see her before she was moved, I just popped into the Edina hospital the next chance I got, without any regard to hours. I got there late at night. I wondered whether Deb would even be awake at that hour.

Deb was reclining in the same little bed in the same room that she had occupied before all of the tests and exploratory surgery. But she didn't look the same. She was well wrapped and secured in the bed, so that she couldn't move around much. Her head was heavily bandaged.

She didn't seem much like the old Deb, either. It took her a moment to realize that I had approached her. I reached for her hand. Then she tried to smile, but it wasn't much of a smile.

"Hi," she said. "Feeling pretty weak just now."

I looked at her for a moment to connect. I struggled for the right words.

"What did they tell you?" I started slowly.

"They operated, but didn't get it all," she said.

"Anything I can bring you?" I asked. "They're moving you to another hospital - Saint Joseph's, for treatment. That's near our home, you know."

"Ah, yes," she said. "I love our house. I want to go back to our house."

"That's why they are starting treatments," I said. "We'll see if we can get you back home."

"That would be nice," she said.

"So, what do you want me to bring you?" I repeated. "Anything?"

"Don't let them take my car," she said. "Take care of my car."

I saw her purse nearby and looked inside.

"You still have your keys," I said. "We won't let anyone take your car. I'll watch your things for you. Don't worry."

"Good," she said.

"So, is there any food or books or something that you want me to bring you? Anything from home?"

"Pizza," she said. "And coffee."

"Okay, you got it."

"I'm tired," Deb said.

I said my goodbyes and left shortly. It struck me that Deb had not asked about Willow, whereas the missing cat was foremost in her mind the last time I had seen her. It occurred to me that nothing would ever be quite the same again.

The next morning, they moved Deb into Saint Joseph's Hospital near our home where they would administer the cancer treatment. Nobody liked to call it chemotherapy, because we had all heard the horror stories about chemo and radiation. This route was painful and a last-ditch effort, and apparently the success rate was low. If this was a slow march toward death, it didn't feel much like a march with dignity.

St. Joseph's Hospital made sense in many ways. It was my understanding that Deb had been raised Catholic. She had hinted to me that she was a lapsed Catholic with little regret for abandoning an active religious life within the Church. The way Deb had explained it to me during our kitchen coffee klatches or during commercial breaks during Star Trek was that she had discovered a new, more personal spiritual outlook that precluded organized religion. So, she looked at the Church as something that she had experienced as a young girl as part of her early upbringing in a Catholic family.

Still, we were glad that Deb had landed at St. Joseph's, getting professional medical treatment that held our only promise for her at the moment. It had a good reputation and was convenient for most of us to visit.

They transferred Deb in a wheel chair and ambulance from Fairview South to St. Joseph's. Sandra called me with the news that Deb had been quickly transferred by ambulance and was already in her bed there. Sandra gave me the room and floor number along with visiting hours.

Consequently, I was able to visit her on her first night in the strange, new surroundings.

The first thing I noticed there was that it wasn't a surgery area, but a regular hospital room of some comfortable size. Deb shared the large room with another patient; and there was a good distance between them. Deb's bed was bigger than the one in Fairview's cancer ward, with more bells and whistles to allow adjustments to her comfort level as needed. The room was generally cheery; and the mood of the staff on that floor seemed upbeat. I took this as a good sign for Deb and her recovery.

To Deb's delight, I had brought a pizza with me, one with everything on it from Domino's take-out store. Her eyes widened instantly upon the presentation of the pizza box. I let her take a slice out of the box on her own; and she did this with ease. It was probably a tasty change from hospital food.

She thanked me for remembering the pizza, so I showed her the thermos of coffee that I had also brought.

"Whoo-hoo!" she exclaimed.

I poured out a cup of black coffee made from ground beans in her own grinder at our house and set it on the table next to her. She was absorbed fully in the pizza. When I held the coffee up to her lips, she was able to grasp the hot cup carefully and guide it to her mouth. Her strength after the surgery surprised me.

"Mmmm!" she commented on the coffee. "Good coffee."

"Should be," I said. "You chose it; and I used your grinder."

She handed the cup back to me after just a couple of swallows.

"So, when do you start the treatments?" I asked.

"Not looking forward to that at all," Deb said. "Thought all that was behind me. I dunno. Tomorrow, I think. Get 'em over with and go home. I miss our Victorian home."

A nurse came into the room and took away the food tray in front of Deb. I set extra pieces of pizza on the little table beside her bed.

"More where that came from," I told Deb, pointing to the pizza.

The nurse looked a little annoyed at the pizza, but let it go.

"So, is this your boyfriend?" she asked Deb.

Deb smiled with a flash of wide eyes. She just looked at me.

"Is it?" the nurse teased.

Deb nodded yes.

166

I wasn't, of course, but was happy that Deb felt she had someone in her corner. I didn't know whether her young boyfriend had visited. I wondered whether her own family had visited that day.

I looked a little nervously around the room. It was so very white. The overhead fluorescent lights were pretty stark. I wished that she had softer light – real sunlight ideally. What would the old Indian gentleman on the phone have said about this lighting, I wondered.

I noticed that very little natural sunlight came into the room, with the shades over the windows. And the air was stale in the way hospitals sometimes smell.

"Say, is there anyway Deb could get a little more sunlight into the room here?" I asked the nurse. "And maybe crack a window slightly, so she gets some fresh air, too?"

The nurse gave me a quick once-over, as though she was sizing me up as a potential trouble-maker.

"We know what's best for Deb," she said. "She needs plenty of rest."

The nurse dimmed the overhead lights.

"She needs to sleep now," she said. "She has a big day tomorrow."

I felt that I had overstayed my welcome.

167

"I know that convalescent centers and health retreats in the past would put people outside in the fresh air and sunlight for natural recovery," I said. Immediately, I wished that I had bit my tongue. I felt that I had said too much and didn't want the nurse on our case here.

"You can come visit her tomorrow," the nurse said. "We'll take good care of her tonight."

Yeah, I thought to myself. There is no sunlight anyway. The sun had already set. I just didn't know what else to do for her.

"I'll bring you more pizza and coffee tomorrow, if you like," I told Deb, inching toward the door to leave.

"That would be nice," Deb said, raising one hand slightly.

In the coming days, I visited Deb at the hospital, each time bringing a new pizza. I brought coffee, too. But when the treatments started, she was too weak to hold the coffee cup to her lips without spilling. And she had lost her taste for pizza, although she always accepted one piece and held it without taking many bites.

The treatments were wearing her down.

I called Sandra for any information she might have and to share my impressions with her.

"A number of people from work have dropped by to see Deb there," Sandra said. "And, of course, Anita and I have been by to see her, too."

"What about her boyfriend?" I asked. "And her family."

"Yeah, I don't know about the boyfriend. I don't think he's been over to see her at all. He might not even know she's in the hospital. And I don't know how to contact him. Do you?"

I said no. I don't even know his name.

"Someone said they saw Deb with a young guy that last day when she went to Bobar's Drug Store. I thought maybe it was her son. But maybe it was the boyfriend."

"What about her family?" I asked. "Have they been up to the hospital since she was moved there for treatment?"

"I don't know. I never run into them. None of the people from work say they run into anyone visiting Deb when they stop by."

We agreed to maintain contact. It might not be Deb's final move. It all depended on the treatments; and her doctors at Fairview hadn't sounded optimistic.

I started to go through Deb's things to see whether I could find something that she might want me to bring. I couldn't imagine what she might like, but I felt that I needed to be prepared to help anyway I could.

Ordinarily, I wouldn't go into a roommate's personal space and go through personal things. But I felt that somebody should do so in Deb's case. I just couldn't put my finger on what I was looking for there.

In her coat closet, I found no fewer than seven of those red Lancôme blazers that she wore to work at the cosmetics counter. They were all in a neat row in the closet.

On a little desk in her bedroom I found receipts from the clinic where she visited regularly for routine tests to determine that she was still cancer-free. And, yes, the last visit only weeks earlier did not include a CAT scan. I wondered whether I should scoop up the reports from the clinic. Curiously, the clinic wasn't far from our house, located on University Avenue.

Her jade necklace was still hanging over her stereo. Everything was just as she had left it, when we called her downstairs to put her in the hospital. I wondered whether I should leave everything in her room the same. Would she be coming back? It was a creepy thought.

Downstairs, I looked in the living room for her things. Wizard's toy box, the wicker basket that matched her wicker rocker and wicker foot rest, was filled with catnip mice and little balls. On the bookshelf, I notice that she had inserted only one book into our household library collection. It was a hardbound address book. Inside was only one listing for someone that I believed was her young son. The address was in Minneapolis. It was in Deb's neat handwriting with the big loops and happy, large letters.

I wondered whether anyone had told her son. I didn't have his phone number, either. The only phone number I had was for her parents in Forest Lake east of town.

I found myself driving over to Minneapolis into a neighborhood that I did not know, with Deb's address book beside me in my little, red Pontiac LeMans. After I parked the car in front of the correct address, I stopped a minute to examine the address book. It was beautiful with a heavy plastic covering and a lovely landscape painting. I figured that Deb would want her son to have it.

I knocked on the door to the house. It wasn't a big house or fancy house, but a small, white house that looked like many in the old neighborhood.

An older woman came to the door. I guessed that it had been Deb's mother-in-law.

I asked whether Jamie was home. She said no.

I handed her the address book.

This was Deb's address book, I told her. The only listing she elected to put in the book was for Jamie. I figured that he would want it.

She thanked me.

"Deb's cancer returned, you know," I told her.

She nodded her head once, then looked down.

"Anyway, thanks," I said. "Please make sure that he gets the book."

I went home to get ready to visit Deb at the hospital. I knew that she was getting weaker every day, but I decided to pop a frozen pizza into our oven and slide it into a pizza box to bring her anyway. Coffee was out of the question. She couldn't handle it.

The phone rang. It was Sandra.

"The chemo isn't working," she said. "They are trying radiation. You know what that is? They bombard her with radiation to try to kill the cancer cells."

"Does that work?" I asked naively.

"Sometimes, I guess. But I hear that it kills all of the cells around it, too. It kills everything. It's a big risk, but what other options does she have?"

She promised to keep me informed. Apparently, she was in communication with Deb's parents and the hospital.

When I got to the hospital, my timing was off. They told me that Deb was coming out of radiation treatment and directed me where to find her.

A nurse was wheeling Deb out of the treatment area. Deb was slumped over in the wheelchair.

"How you doin' today?" I asked her.

Slowly she looked up.

"I feel really sick," was all she said. She looked down vacantly.

"Stay strong," I advised. "Keep on fighting."

The nurse started to wheel her back to her room. I followed them down the hall to Deb's room.

"Deb's had a difficult day," she said. "Radiation takes a lot out of you. It makes you sick."

Sandra was in Deb's room when we got there.

We took turns sitting by Deb's bed once she was slowly placed there. We tried holding her hand. Her grip was pretty weak.

After a couple of minutes, I announced that I probably should go. I stood outside Deb's room until Sandra came out. I didn't have to wait long.

"Tell me," I asked Sandra, "is Deb getting any more visitors now? I'm sure word has gotten out."

"It's pretty much just the same core group from work. People who knew Deb from work. I think her parents visited earlier today, but I'm not sure. Whenever I come, there's nobody here."

"Well, I'm glad that people from work are coming. She needs support."

Sandra nodded.

"Deb was telling me just before the intervention that she was fighting with a co-worker and not getting along at work."

"That was me," Sandra said. "Just me. Only me. Deb was mad at me."

"Because you got to wear the lab coat; and Deb was stuck behind the counter alone?"

"Yeah. Something like that. Hey, you got to realize that Deb had worked there a long time. They didn't pay her well or anything. But thank goodness they're covering all of this medical expense."

"That's wonderful," I agreed. "They're paying everything?"

"Full coverage - whatever is needed, is what personnel told me. They are standing by her."

Walking to my car, however, I had to wonder if every little thing would be covered or whether her parents would get stuck with some co-pay. Cancer treatment can't be cheap.

A couple of days later, Sandra called me to say that the radiation wasn't working. Apparently, the cancer had spread too much. The decision was made to find Deb a bed somewhere. I wasn't involved. They no longer asked for my input.

I asked what kind of bed and what they were looking for next.

"It's pretty much the end of the line," Sandra said. "They are recommending hospice."

I reminded her that we'd already done the exercise back at Fairview South and had concluded that we didn't have enough people with enough time to provide home care for Deb.

"We're looking for a hospice center," Sandra said. "But it's hard to find a bed. Because Deb's family apparently is Catholic, we probably could get her into the place on Saint Anthony Way near your house – Sisters of Perpetual Care of something like that. It's on that frontage road that runs just north of Highway 94 in Saint Paul."

"Perfect location," I said.

"Yeah, but there's a waiting list. We have to find a place to stash Deb while she waits for a bed to open up."

"Stash her?"

"There's a rehab center that works with cancer patients. It's called Sister Kenny's. Ever hear of it? It's famous. Anyway, they'd take her."

175

"Rehabilitation?" I asked.

"Well, that's the story we'll use to get her in there."

Things were moving quickly - too quickly for Deb. It was only a few weeks since the intervention that brought her to Fairview South; and the medical community was already giving up on her.

St. Joseph's released her quickly and transported her to Sister Kenny's. They welcomed her without question and with great enthusiasm. The staff there was dedicated to making life as livable as possible for people, no matter what their condition suggested.

As soon as I arrived for a visit, a rehab therapist took me on a tour through the room where Deb would receive personal training to strengthen her body and cope with daily situations, like the use of a telephone.

She showed me the parallel bars that they would ask Deb to negotiate and the various household situations that they had simulated to help a person adapt to living at home again.

Admittedly, it was hard to sound enthusiastic and promising to help Deb adapt to the rehab program. In effect, I was lying to the physical therapist in assuring her that I would help Deb make a successful return to home. She wouldn't have the strength to pull her weakened body through the parallel bars. She wouldn't be able to operate a phone or a kitchen stove again. All of her friends and family knew that; and we all probably went through the same lies over at Sister Kenny's. Nonetheless, the staff was optimistically doing all that they could to re-orient and strengthen Deb to return to her old life. It just wasn't going to happen; and we never really were honest with the good people at Sister Kenny's.

Just the same, I did come down to visit Deb at the rehab center one day when they were running her through the drills. It was sad to watch. No, she couldn't work her way down the parallel bars. She tried to dial 911 on the disconnected rotary phone in the rehab room, with a lot of prompting from the therapist. At last she dialed the three numbers and seemed to take great comfort in finally succeeding in dialing the phone correctly. Everything that Deb attempted to do in the rehab room, however, was beyond her ability. She just didn't have it within her anymore. She couldn't even speak properly after all of the chemo and radiation treatments. Deb was a shell of a person; and it was so sad to see. Here was a young woman of 32 years old who really wanted to live, a person who had fought to overcome cancer and gone through an eight-year remission.

Knowing that she wouldn't be there any longer than it took for a bed to become available at a hospice center, her friends all skipped most of her rehab sessions. We really didn't know how our being there would make a difference, as there would be no recovery. Speaking only for myself, I think I went only one other time.

The physical therapist who worked with Deb jumped me on my second visit for not participating and helping Deb in her rehabilitation. She pointed out that I would need to work with her, if she was going to make a successful return to our house and begin using the phone and the stove at our house. As a result, she said, the rehab center couldn't keep her there much longer, since nobody was getting involved with Deb's rehab.

A panic ran through my body. If we couldn't keep Deb at Sister Kenny's until a hospice bed became available, what would we do? Where would we bring her?

I vowed to come back regularly and become more active in her rehabilitation exercises.

Chapter 9
November–December 1992

The next day, fortunately, Sandra called me with the good news that a hospice center had found room for Deb. Of course, the sudden availability of a bed at the hospice center could only mean that somebody had recently died there.

The hospice was so tucked away in a corner of Saint Paul that I actually drove past the place on my first attempt to find it. It was a long, brick building near Cleveland on St. Anthony Way, a highway frontage road that just blended into the landscape like a nondescript industrial storage building or something. There was a parking space tucked against one side of the building.

The bedding arrangement at Our Lady of Good Counsel looked very different from the previous hospital and rehab center patient facilities. The beds basically were lined up in one row on either side of a long aisle. The place was filled with wall-to-wall beds. A number of Catholic nuns served as nurses for these terminally ill patients. The place was startling in its quietness. Few patients showed any sort of movement. Most were sleeping. The nurses passed through the building on their many rounds efficiently and quietly, administering to the sick all around them.

Most impressive was the openness of the facility, with nobody walled away in small, isolated rooms. Also striking was the abundance of light in the brick building. Unlike the hospitals where Deb had been, this hospice facility had plenty of windows without drapes or shades to block the natural sunlight. The light from outside sprayed across the facility from the many high windows and lit up the building.

My familiarity with hospice was limited to the Mount Hood Hospice in Sandy, Oregon. I was a volunteer with the small, non-profit group briefly when I published the newspaper in Sandy. We provided the group with space in the back of our newspaper building, once the commercial printing presses there were removed. This little Mount Hood hospice program, on the other hand, sent nurses and volunteers to care for people in their homes and did not provide resident boarding. Seeing so many dying people lined neatly in long rows of beds was something totally new and humbling to me.

Our Lady of Good Counsel offered free hospice care and specialized in end-of-life care for cancer patients.

Since I had never visited this charitable organization before, I thought it appropriate that I should check into the office before visiting Deb. The building was all white inside with many alcoves, nooks, hallways, and ante-rooms in addition to the main bedding area. The office was located at the far end of the building. As I passed down the aisle, I looked from side to side to try to find Deb in one of the beds. She was on the right side and sleeping quietly when I passed her.

The door to the office was open, but I knocked anyway.

A young nun, dressed in an odd outfit that was part religious habit and half nurse's uniform, stood up behind her desk, which faced the door. Part of her uniform – her hat, showed that she was a nun, while the rest of the uniform looked to be basically a white nurse's outfit. I noticed that she had an easy smile and quiet demeanor but was decidedly business-like and in charge here.

We introduced ourselves. In so doing, I told her everything that Deb had gone through, about the pointless, painful radiation and chemotherapy that she had endured at my suggestion. I even told the sister about the awkward stint we put Deb through at Sister Kenny's, just to stall long enough for a hospice bed to become available. I told her about Deb's earlier bout with cancer and how she had miraculously recovered and gone through eight years of glorious remission. And I told her how a book had featured Deb's story of recovery and how Deb had gone on the radio with the author to tell her story.

The sister patiently listened to all of that and then just looked deeply into my eyes.

"Deb's job now is to die," she told me. "That's why she's here. We will try to make that death as peaceful and easy as possible. And, of course, you can help."

I told the sister about Deb's friends from work and family who would also be dropping by. She said that she had already met some of them, and that all of them were welcome most any time.

"Tell me, now," she said. "Is Deb a Catholic?"

I swallowed hard. Deb and I had spoken about her spiritual beliefs. I knew that she was no longer a practicing Catholic, but apparently had been raised in a traditional Catholic family.

"Not anymore, I guess," I told the sister. "I believe that Deb was raised Catholic. She probably hasn't been a practicing Catholic in some time, however. Like a lot of young people today, Deb's idea of spirituality has evolved."

The pretty, young nun with the dark hair smiled at me. I hoped that I hadn't disqualified Deb from their care or put her into another category of consideration as a patient there.

"Well, we are all Catholic when we die, aren't we?" she said softly.

I pondered that. It was a magnanimous view, I suppose. It was most certainly inclusive. But I wondered whether she meant catholic with a lower-case C. Probably. That implied universality or part of a whole, as opposed to members or participants in the Holy Church of Rome.

This was a smart nun, I quickly surmised, and a caring human being. Yes, she was a genuine nurse who cared for the dying.

She told me that visiting hours were very generous at Our Lady and that friends and family were welcome most anytime when their loved ones were approaching their hour of death.

I indicated that I already knew where Deb's bed was located and would like to spend some time with her now.

"Of course," she said quietly. "And just let me know if you have any questions or concerns along the way. The idea is to make Deb as comfortable and peaceful here as possible. That's what we're all working to achieve."

When I left, I started to close the door to her office. She asked me to leave it wide open. I felt good about this place and was so glad that they had welcomed Deb.

I pulled up a chair beside Deb's bed and waited to see if she would awaken. She looked so very still and restful there in that bed, with her recent bouts with radiation and chemotherapy now behind her. There were no more exercises and drills at the rehab center to worry her.

When I held her hand, her eyes slowly opened. She smiled faintly. Her eyes looked a little brighter today.

"Hi," she said simply. "Thanks for coming."

I asked whether I could bring her anything. She passed on pizza. She passed on magazines.

I suggested a movie or maybe bringing her cat Wizard to visit, if that would be possible.

"Can you do that?" she asked.

I said that I would bring Wizard and we'd find out if the staff had any problems with that, once he was already in the building. My impression was that the staff would be very accommodating.

"How about I bring you a movie tomorrow?"

"Dumb and Dumber," Deb said. "I like that one."

I'd never heard of it but promised to bring her something good.

"So, the people here are pretty nice, right?" I said.

She just smiled.

"I don't know if you noticed," I said, "but this room is very bright and open. And there's a lot of light. They have a lot of windows, and the sunlight is shining through everywhere. There's a big ray of sunlight shining down on your bed right now."

Deb strained in the bed to try to turn her head a little to look around. She still wore the bandages on her head and was pretty immobile.

"Do you remember what I told you about the old man from India who used to call me and tell me about the magic of light?" I asked.

Deb looked blank.

"Well, he told me that if you stood in the light and lived in the light, that you could be transformed. You could actually move in the light, he said. And he said natural sunlight was the best. He also said that every morning brought special sunlight; and that it was good to put yourself in that light."

Seeing that she was weak, tired, and incapable of much conversation, I stood up to leave. I promised to bring her a movie tomorrow. And I encouraged her to feel the light all around her. I grabbed my chair to put it back where I'd found it.

Looking back at Deb flat on her back, she looked so alone.

"Hang in there," I said. "Keep fighting."

The next day, I did bring a movie. I rented a special 50th anniversary edition of the MGM re-release of "The Wizard of Oz." It was highly regarded at the time as a newly, retouched film with improved color and sound. It also offered behind-the-scene features about the movie classic. I thought it would be uplifting and maybe bring back happy childhood memories.

Deb didn't look too impressed when I told her that I had the movie, but I pressed on with our private screening. I asked the staff for a TV to play it. My movie rental had included a video player from the video store.

I set it up in the hallway around the corner from Deb's area. There was traffic there, but mostly nurses going about their stations. I put Deb into a wheelchair, which one of the sisters provided. We sat together for about two hours of silence watching the movie together.

Honestly, I don't think Deb enjoyed it much; but plainly there was not much joy anywhere for Deb these days. I put her back into her bed. It was harder than I had imagined, moving her about by myself. But the sisters didn't fuss much about how friends interacted with the people in their care. I was thankful for that.

On one of my next visits, I brought Deb's cat Wizard. The old black cat with long hair was so loving and gentle that he stepped easily into the carrier and then stepped out of the carrier onto her narrow bed when I set the blue crate beside her feet.

Wizard moved softly, but swiftly onto Deb's body, as she lay face-up in the bed. He sat on her chest and looked into her eyes.

186

That brought the most reaction from Deb that I had seen in some time. She reached out to pet him but discovered that she didn't have much hand-eye coordination. So, she just laid her hand upon him; and that seemed fine with Wizard. He sat there quietly without moving a muscle.

Yes, Wizard had been her healer. And he saw that his work was not finished.

Deb moved about more in her bed than she had in days, trying to position her cat in a way that worked well for both of them on that narrow bed.

I asked whether Deb wanted to get into a wheelchair and move around with her cat. She nodded yes with enthusiasm, so I borrowed another wheelchair, leaving the cat on the bed with Deb. When I returned, he was sticking close to her, uninhibited by the strange surroundings and other people there.

I left him on the bed, while I got Deb into the wheelchair. Deb was wearing a white bathrobe. Once she was comfortably in the chair, I set the cat on her lap. I put a leash on him, just in case he got spooked and started to bolt.

We slowly made our way through the facility, going everywhere in the building with the cat who sat motionless on her lap. Deb held the end of the cat's leash in one hand. She moved the leash across his body in the only way to pet him that she felt able to do. I was surprised that he liked that. Somehow, he seemed to know that it was the only way she was able to pet him at the moment. He was purring and looked into her face with great devotion and love.

When I put Deb back into her bed, I set the cat on the bed with her. Again, Deb clutched the cat's leash, although it was clear from his demeanor that he was not going anywhere.

After setting the side rails up on her bed, I returned the wheelchair back to the nun who had found it for me. In that hallway, I saw an outside door open and another wheelchair burst into the building. This wheelchair held a patient who was being pushed by a family member or friend. They seemed to be having a good time on their little outing.

After they had passed me, I asked the nun there whether I could take Deb outside in a wheelchair.

"Oh, yes!" she said cheerfully. "Many people do that; and we're fine with that. Just let us know where you are going and when you will return. You know, a lot of men – older men, like to push them around outside. And they go fast, too. Anyway, that's the way they seem to deal with it. Racing down the road in the wheelchair with the wind in their faces. It's almost like they can push back death. Well, we all do the best we can, of course. And the people here like to get outside from time to time, too."

That got me thinking. I wasn't thinking about a wheelchair race down the sidewalk with the leaves flying all around us. The next day was Saturday; and I could spend the afternoon with Deb on an outing. I tried to think of someplace interesting. She had spoken often about her summer camp outs at We Fest summer music festival outside of town. It was an outdoors country music festival with camping on a ranch by the water near Detroit Lakes. Taking her there was out of the question. Then again, maybe a trip to our local zoo would be fun for her. Our Como Zoo was located in a big, rustic park nearby. It was open even in the fall and winter.

After clearing my plan with the staff, I bundled Deb in warm clothes and put her into the wheel chair. I could see that her catheter bag would be a problem, as she flinched whenever anything came into contact with it. Of course, the bag was attached directly to her body, which was naturally sensitive.

I should have brought her one of her snappy hats, since the season was changing quickly with fall upon us and winter dead ahead. Then, again, it was a chance for her to show off her long, golden hair, since the shortened schedule of radiation hadn't claimed much of it. Once we got outside, the cool late fall air seemed to bring a little color back into her cheeks once we were outdoors. She squinted her eyes in the sunlight outdoors. A gentle breeze blew her fine blond hair across her face. I put my stocking cap atop her head just to keep her warm.

Getting her into the car proved difficult, because she needed a lot of help to move from the wheelchair to my car's front seat. I wished that I'd had a wheelchair-accessible van; but made the best of things anyway. Fortunately, her wheel chair folded neatly to fit into the car's trunk.

We did not speak much on the trip. Deb's speech was quickly deteriorating, as she grew weaker and fainter every day now. But I tried to keep up a cheerful banter, as we rolled down the road. I told her about people and conditions at the house.

On the way to the Como Park Zoo, I drove us past our house and pointed out that her red car was still safely parked beside the house. She showed no emotion on seeing the car or the house.

Parking as close to the zoo as possible, I chose a spot for the car at the edge of the lot, so that I could maneuver Deb out of the car and into the wheelchair with little interference. I bumped the catheter again; and she winced. I made a mental note to be much more careful about that in the future.

Together we wheeled our way throughout the entire zoo. On that crisp autumn afternoon, the zoo was pretty much deserted – the two of us, a lot of lonely animals, and a few other lost people who wandered about, wondering why so many of the concession shops were closed that time of year.

We went into a dark cavern that housed the monkeys and great apes. We saw the marine animals. Even the giraffe came out to see us. Our journey took us literally around the entire zoo. Deb seemed to hold up well, although she showed little enthusiasm. There was no joy left.

Back at Our Lady, I put Deb back into her bed and returned the wheelchair. One of the sisters asked me how things had gone. I simply told her that Deb held up well and that we experienced no problems.

Well, it was not exactly Star Trek or camping at the We Fest. But at least Deb got some fresh air and a clear, sunny day outdoors. Like the rest of her friends, I suspect, I was doing the best that I could to ease her transition from life into death. It wasn't easy. And it wasn't enough.

Chapter 10
Mid-December 1992

Sandra called to ask how I thought Deb was doing. I told her about taking Deb out to the Como Zoo; and I was happily surprised to learn from Sandra that Deb's father also had taken her on a wheelchair ride around the block a couple of times. Apparently, he was one of those people that the sister was talking about, older men who put so much faith in just getting outside and racing against the wind. I'm sure he was heartbroken about his Debbie and wanted to push back the inevitable as much as anyone.

Sandra asked me whether I thought the sisters at the hospice center were primarily nuns or primarily nurses. As grateful as we were to Our Lady of Good Counsel for taking Deb into their facility, I could understand exactly what Sandra meant. I had wondered the same. Was Deb getting good nursing or simply good counseling? I told Sandra that I was impressed by the staff at Our Lady and found them to be totally dedicated. But the question did fester in me.

On my next visit, I stopped by the office after seeing Deb to try to see the head nurse. Looking her over carefully, I couldn't get over how diminutive she was, despite her bold confidence. She looked so young and fragile. A little wisp of fine black hair fell from under her nun's cap on one side, no doubt oblivious to her. As always, she displayed a pleasant and accommodating demeanor. She asked me whether I had a question or a concern.

I thanked her for everything that she and her staff had been doing for Deb since we arrived and then asked whether I could ask her a somewhat personal question.

She looked puzzled, but softly asked me to close the door for a moment.

"I feel a little awkward asking you such a question, Sister," I said, "but it's just something that I feel I have to ask you. And you don't have to answer, of course. Excuse me for being so forward..."

"That's alright," she said quietly. "What's on your mind?"

"It's obvious to anyone that you do an incredible job here running this place in your role as a nurse and also as a nun," I said a little haltingly, averting my eyes. "I'm just wondering, do you see yourself first and foremost as nun or primarily as a nurse?"

I looked up into her eyes to read her response.

"A nurse," she answered quickly. "I see myself as first a nurse and then as a nun. But being a nun here gives me a special opportunity as a nurse. Was that all that you wanted to ask me?"

I thanked her and left. Remembering her policy, I left her door open.

In those December days of darkness with shortened daylight, I found it harder and harder to shovel the walkways and then make it over to the hospice center after work. There literally weren't enough hours in my day.

One night, I lay down on my back in my bed thinking about going to the hospice center. I'd just shoveled the sidewalks and steps and was dog tired and dirty. By the time I had changed clothes, I realized that I was late and would probably miss seeing her before she went to sleep. I rushed out the front door and dashed down the stairs, only to skid on a new coat of snow that had formed. I grabbed for the hand rail, but I had already started to fall down the flight of cement stairs. Once back on my feet, I found it difficult and sore to walk, but I knew that my opportunities to visit Deb were fleeting. I hopped into the little Pontiac LeMans and drove the three miles to Our Lady just before the they started to put the place to bed for the night.

I sat beside Deb and tried to get her to talk. It was becoming impossible for her to articulate anything that she wanted to express, although you could see in her alert eyes that she still had a lot of awareness.

"Whoo!" she said. "Whoo-hoo!" she said again.

She smiled a silly little smile, as though she knew that her utterance sounded silly.

"Whoo-hoo to you, too," I said, patting one of her hands. Her hands felt clammy.

"Listen," I said. "I've been thinking of what we can try doing to make things a little more comfortable for you here," I said. "Would you like some massage? Or energy work? Or we could try working with light."

Her eyes opened wider.

"OK," I said. "We'll see what we can do. Meanwhile, you hang in there, okay? Keep fighting."

Later that night I called Sandra and asked how she felt about trying some alternative energy healing exercises on Deb. I suggested massage or some form alternative health practice. A lot of modalities in the hands-on healing arts came to my mind once I started talking about the possibilities.

"Actually, a few other people have dropped by and tried something like that," Sandra said. "People at work are thinking the same thing and have brought a few energy healers up to see her. I guess we're at the desperation point now. There's nothing medical science can do for her or will do for her."

"Yeah," I agreed. "But I just feel like I have to try. Maybe I'll try something different."

After my next visit to Deb, I saw in one of the magazines that we got at work where some doctor in California had concocted a mixture of green herbs that prepared properly might control and even reverse cancer. Or that's what his advertisement in the magazine suggested, at least. What did I have to lose?

Well, I had $100 to lose on the ingredients – just a few bags of herbs and a server. Plus, shipping costs. But I was willing to try anything. There were no other viable options.

I noticed that the herbs had to be prepared in a certain manner over heat at midnight. I thought that a little strange and a bit "witchy." When I mentioned that to my publisher, who had a background in witchcraft, high magic, and herbalism, he agreed that it sounded like a magical formula. He said that the instructions to begin mixing and heating the herbs at exactly midnight was a dead giveaway that it was a magical brew.

The herbs were common garden variety herbs, or weeds in some eyes. They were wild herb plants that you could cook to a dark, green substance. The cooking however, left them stringy and fibrous in texture, no matter how long I seem to run everything through the blender. The Native herbalist who taught me that weeds in nature could have nutritional, and even medicinal value when cooked in a pot evidently never tried running what she lovingly called "green pot herbs" through a blender.

Staying up until one o'clock in the morning was the real difficulty in the preparation. I had to get up pretty early for work the next morning.

The applicator for the magical brew was a clear plastic bottle with a built-in straw that looked more like a nipple. The cup sealed tightly. Anyway, the idea was to set it into somebody's mouth without any spillage.

Of course, I tasted it before serving it. Frankly, it didn't do anything for me, but then I didn't have terminal cancer. No, it did not taste good, but was not as foul as some medicines. It was a cocktail of natural herbs.

When I presented it to Deb, I suggested that she could try it, if she wanted. I explained the idea behind it and where I had found it. She reached out to try to grab it. To assist her, I positioned the bottle in her mouth and held it at a downward tilt for her. I watched carefully for her reaction. She got half of it down. That was a good effort, I thought. It was a valiant try.

But even the optimistic ad in the magazine indicated that the herbal formula would work best in cases where the cancer was not advanced. So, we couldn't expect miracles, even if the product was any good.

I continued to bring the green milkshake in the clear plastic bottle for Deb during the next several days. After a while, though, she rejected it. I put it away and never offered it to her again. I really didn't expect a miracle, a reversal of fortunes. Results in some cases with this herbal blend were found in seven days, according to the good doctor's ad. We'd given it about a weak. Clearly, this case was different.

I entered the hospice center with its big cross at the entrance on the next day, bringing with me only the snow that clung to my coat and hat. It was getting blustery outdoors and plenty cold and dreary. I wondered whether Deb would make it to the spring, so I could take her outdoors again on a pleasant, sunny day.

I had managed to get there at a late afternoon hour when things were slowed down a bit. Apparently, I caught the facility between meals and routine rounds for medication. Nuns who nursed the dying there responded to patients who would cry or call out; but that rarely happened, it seemed.

On this afternoon, I observed the sisters participating quietly throughout the building in prayers to observe Stations of the Cross. Apparently, there was a designated hour for all of them to do that en mass, because I noticed nuns throughout the entire building kneeling silently at the same time, wherever they happened to be at that time. Some were in doorways. Some were in hallways. All of them were kneeling on the ground in silent prayers to observe the suffering and death of Jesus Christ. It was pretty moving.

During their observance of Stations of the Cross, however, I heard a patient in one of the beds calling out. Nonetheless, all of the nuns continued praying. I had to wonder whether the sisters would ignore a dying patient during this ritual. It sort of festered in me, thinking about Deb who could not speak, but could only utter a little howl. What if she needed urgent attention? Would one of the sisters come to her aid when needed, or ignore her during their hour of prayer?

I sat a while with Deb and then asked her to excuse me for a minute. I made my way into the office to speak to the head nurse about my concern.

She was pouring over her busy desk when I knocked on the frame of her open door. She motioned for me to come inside and then stood up, offering me her full and immediate attention.

"Sorry to bother you, Sister," I said, "but I did have a question, if you don't mind."

"Of course," she said.

"I notice that the sisters all kneel at the same time of day in observance of the Stations of the Cross. I understand that it's important, but..."

"Was there something that you wanted to know about it?" she asked.

"Well," I started again, "I was just wondering if everything stops here during Stations of the Cross. For instance, if someone needed medication or urgent attention, would that patient be ignored – I mean, postponed, until the observance was over?"

"Oh," she said. "No. Everyone who works here is very dedicated. We have taken vows. We are here to serve. If someone needed our care urgently, a sister would attend to him, of course. And then she would return to her prayers when she had an opportunity. Our patients come first here. Always."

My admiration for this nurse who served as a nun grew daily. She was calm, thoughtful, and concerned. Deb couldn't ask for a better professional to care for her in her dying hours.

Back at Deb's bedside, I leaned over to see if Deb was sleeping or just drowsy. Sometimes lately it was hard to tell. I finally decided that she was awake.

"Hey, there," I said. "I'm back. Miss me?"

Her gaze was rather vacant, but her eyes did open a little wider.

"Are you hanging in there?" I asked. "Keep fighting, okay? This isn't over yet."

I noticed that the light from one of the windows was now streaming across the foot of her bed.

"Do you remember our talks about light and how light can magically transform us? It can take us beyond time and space, you know. And look at all the amazing light that you have on you now. There's a shaft of beautiful sunlight streaming down on your bed."

Deb strained to try to see the light at the bottom half of the bed. This seemed to interest her.

"This is a wonderful place here," I said. "The sisters who watch over you really do care. It's a nourishing environment. And everyone here is behind you one-hundred percent. They have your best interest at heart. I just spoke to the head nurse. She's a warm and loving person. I'm so glad we found this place for you. So just rest and know that you are loved. Okay?"

She was listening. That level of involvement was rare these days.

"Yes," I continued, "that old Indian gentleman told me a lot about light. It's pretty amazing, really. Every living thing from the sun to the center of the earth, including us, is blessed by light energy. It nourishes us and energizes us. We absorb, process, and transform this light as radiant energy. Without light, we are nothing. And if we could live in the light and move in the light, this energy could take us anywhere at the speed of light. We could travel beyond the limits of this physical world that grounds us and holds us fast. We could move freely like light anywhere and anytime. Time and space would be no barrier to us. Our consciousness would merge with the light and flow freely. We would be beyond pain and suffering, beyond life and death. We would become light, fully transformed."

Her eyes widened and focused on me squarely.

"That's what we want for you," I said. "Freedom from pain and freedom from what holds you back. Light never dies. It continues on a direct course until it reaches its destination. Then it's absorbed, processed, and transferred. No matter how dark things might appear at time, there is always light. And it seeks us out."

I spoke about the ray of creation and the seven rays of light. I spoke about the seven angels of the presence as seven rays of light. I told her about the many references to god as light. And I described the life-generating and sustaining qualities of light.

"Your consciousness, the divine spirit in you that burns like a spark, is part of this light," I told her. "Your inner being, your life force is radiant energy, just the same as light. So if you merge with the light, you can move with the light. Doesn't that seem reasonable?" I asked. "Or does it sound like Star Trek? Remember, they could re-materialize anywhere on Star Trek. Doesn't that sound a little like moving with the light? Or do you remember Star Wars, and the Force? Surely, there is a life force that directs all of life. That life force is part of you.

"The only thing that's holding you back now," I said to Deb, "is your decaying body. Everything inside of you that really matters – your divine spirit, your essential life force, your spark of life - is strong and everlasting. Nothing can destroy your life force. It's pure energy and will live forever. That's a promise."

Her eyes and wrinkled forehead indicated that she was absorbing these words and thinking hard on them.

"A person who lives in the light will never die," I continued. "A person who moves in the light will go forward. It's so easy. You can do that, right?"

She squeezed my hand.

"I will be back," I told her. "I will be here to hold your hand and help you move on. Everything is going to be alright. You've got to believe that. Okay?"

She continued holding my hand, as best she could.

"Tomorrow is another day," I said. "The sun will come up and shine on you. You have lots more tomorrows. Don't worry about a thing."

Walking out, I felt that I had to call Sandra. Up until that day, we had uniformly urged Deb to fight and hold on. It occurred to me at last that she must feel boxed in with no place to go. How could she hold onto her fragile physical life, when it was slipping away a little more every day? Maybe it was time for another approach.

Chapter 11
Late December - Early January 1992

My call to Sandra was a little revealing. Yes, apparently everyone had been encouraging Deb to hold on and fight to live, despite the hopeless odds. And now all of her friends, or at least those who visited and spoke with Sandra, were changing their entire attitude about that. Those closest to Deb these days were beginning to sense that it was time to ease her transition and encourage her to let go.

Apparently, that included her family. I got a call right from Deb's mother right after speaking with Sandra. Her mother wanted to set up a time to drop by and pick up Deb's things.

It seemed like a logical request, but it upset me on a couple of levels. Deb was still very much alive and struggling day to day just down the road from our house. It seemed odd to me that her things would be snapped up and tossed, boxed, or redistributed while she was still alive and technically still a resident at our Victorian home. It also bothered me to think how her parents had never visited Deb at her Victorian home in the six months that she had lived there. Of course, I was out of town on business several weeks during that period, but I never heard about a visit. Deb never seemed to receive visitors at the house. Now her parents wanted to visit her house to clear her things out. The trip made logical sense, but it seemed callous to me.

Her parents, on the other hand, were very kind and considerate when they did visit the house to collect Deb's things. I supposed that they were pleasant to me as a way of making the difficult situation - the ripping away of everything that was Deb in our house, as seamless as possible.

They went through Deb's bedroom and the rest of the house carefully to identify things that belonged to Deb. In the bedroom, of course, everything there belonged to Deb. They made mental notes of what items were involved and discussed what to do about all of them. Deb's mother seemed to take the lead and dictate how to handle each item, asking her husband only for his agreement to her assessment.

"Who should get the stereo and television?" she asked him. Before he could formulate an answer, she came up with the name of a relative who would inherit them.

Next, they took measure of Deb's little writing desk and what they might do with that. They decided fairly quickly where to move them, and then considered Deb's chairs.

Deb's mother told her husband that some things would need to be decided later and that they would simply take these items home to distribute later.

Deb had a collection of music; and that was pledged to the young woman who would receive her stereo. I didn't ask but assumed that the recipient was a younger sister or cousin.

Next, her mother examined the big jade necklace that I had given to Deb. It was still hung over her stereo in a decorative fashion.

"Huh," her mother commented. "Nice."

She looked at the larger table in Deb's bedroom, the table that had once been Deb's kitchen table when she had her own apartment with another young woman before moving to our Victorian house.

"You can have that table," she told me, pointing to the vinyl kitchen table. "If you want it, I mean. I'd rather not take it. Don't know what to do with it. So much stuff. We don't have that much space to move everything."

I told her that I understood and that I'd be glad to keep the table there in the room.

Deb's mother opened up the clothes closet to examine the contents. She worked her way through the many red Lancôme Paris blazers that Deb had accumulated from work, somewhat amazed that there were so many of them. She looked into the shelves at Deb's other clothes, including her signature hats.

She commented that a sister or cousin might make use of them. She said they'd have to determine where they went later. It was hard to tell, she said, adding that they might not even be wanted.

She pulled a few pictures off the wall. They were not pictures of family or friends, but of birds. She set them on Deb's table, as though not to forget them when packing up.

"Did she have anything anywhere else in the house?" she asked me.

I indicated that Deb had things in the bathroom, living room, laundry room, and kitchen.

Her mother said that she wasn't much concerned about items in the bathroom or laundry, unless I wanted them removed. I told her that everything was okay there, as far as I was concerned. I didn't want Deb totally out of the house, not anytime soon. I liked the idea of her hairbrush in the bathroom and her favorite soap in the laundry room.

We moved into the living room. Deb's parents surveyed the room. There were little pieces of Deb's life, values, and lifestyle all over the room.

I pointed out the items in the room that belonged to Deb, without commenting on anything. There were large, matching wall hangings of animals she loved. There was a matching set of tigers and a matching set of domestic kittens. These pictures looked old and had probably decorated Deb's many homes over the years. They were framed in large wooden frames. Deb's wicker rocker still stood in front of the television. The matching foot stool and matching wicker basket that held all of Wizard's toys also adorned the room.

Her parents had no interest in the pictures of animals. Deb's mother suggested that the wicker furniture probably went better in this house than it would look in their home and that my living room might look bare if they removed the pieces.

In the kitchen, we went through our old-style pantry to examine Deb's food. They boxed up some of it. The Dayton clock on the wall over the pantry was something they wanted to leave behind. They also had no interest in her Dayton microwave, noting that we would probably need it at the house there.

I showed them Deb's coffee grinder, one of her most cherish possessions. They waved it off as something insignificant. Apparently, they had one already or else never ground their own coffee. Grinding flavorful coffee each new day was a way of life with their daughter.

They took a few things from the kitchen, but very little.

Walking to the door, they whispered between themselves about which family members would get what things when they loaded up Deb's possessions.

Deb's mother surprised me at the door by offering to pay Deb's rent, if she was not current. I pointed out that Deb had not lived at the house in recent months. She asked again whether Deb was current when she left the house. I told her that Deb's last rent check had bounced, but that it was okay.

She reached into her purse to retrieve a check book. She asked how much that amount was. I told her that it was only $295 and to let it go. She pointed out that Deb's things had remained in her bedroom since her departure and said that she would pay me for two months. I was a little flabbergasted by her generosity and thanked her for the check.

Then she asked me for the keys to Deb's car out front. Remembering my promise to Deb, which made little sense at this late date, I balked.

"I don't have the keys," I said truthfully, remembering full well that they rested dormant in Deb's purse. I felt a little shamed to block their efforts to get the car, since Deb would never drive it again and Deb had told me that her father helped her get the car, so he was clearly invested in the car.

"No matter," Deb's mother said. "We have another set of keys, I think." She looked at her husband, who nodded affirmatively.

"Or you can look in Deb's purse at the hospice center," I interjected. "I think she put her car keys there."

At the front door, they negotiated a time to return to pack up the items. It occurred to me that I should help them pack and load, but my heart wasn't in it. Honestly, I didn't even want to be present during the removal of Deb's things. I scheduled a time when I knew that I would be at work, letting them know that I would have another house mate let them into the house.

"If that doesn't work, just look under the doormat for a key," I said. "No problem. I just can't be here myself, since I work at that time."

They told me they understood. Did they? I wondered.

When I came home the next night to get ready to visit Deb, her things were gone. Many of her favorite items in the pantry were gone and some of her pots and pans were missing. I checked her room, and there was little sign that Deb had ever lived there, except for the outline in the carpet left by her furniture, TV and stereo. The cat flap that I had installed at the bottom of the bedroom door was one of the few reminders that Deb had lived there with her cats. Mr. Wizard had continued to go into her bedroom to sleep on Deb's bed at night, as he always had; and I had to wonder how he would react to the disappearance of her bed now.

Deb's dining room table stayed in her room for a long time after that day. And her magnificent wall pictures of tigers and kittens remained, along with her wicker rocker, foot rest, and wicker basket of toys for Wizard.

The clock and microwave remained for some time after that, too, but finally wore down with use. Everything mechanical decays and wears out in time, I suppose – even the human body.

The next day, I visited the hospice center after work as usual. Deb was fading fast. She did not respond immediately to my presence, as though she were a million miles away. When I began to speak to her, however, she swiveled her eyes toward me, without moving her body.

It was impossible for me to realize how much she hurt. And she probably hurt on many levels in addition to the physical discomfort of being immobile and numb. Her decaying body had shrunk. She had always been thin and tall. Now her long body lay limp on the narrow bed like a thin ribbon without much substance at all. She had little appetite or enthusiasm for life remaining. Yet she hung on. She was just shy of her thirty-third birthday; and there was so much she had longed to see and do that would never come her way now. It was easy to understand in spite of everything why she hung on to life. Outside this building, there were a numberless string of easy days of laughter and adventure that would come freely to everyone in the world, except Deb.

"Hey," I said. "How you doing today?"

No response.

"Listen, I said, "I was thinking of bring Wizard to visit you again. You up to that?"

No response.

"He really loves you, you know. He's doing okay, but he would love to come see you."

Deb just stared out into open space, not looking at me any longer.

"I'll go set that up, okay? I'll be right back. I'm going to see the head nurse here."

I squeezed her hand. She did not squeeze back.

My visit to the office was not about the cat. I knew the head nun here would approve of the cat's visit, as long as Wizard were well behaved, as before. But I did want to speak with her about Deb's overall condition and dramatic decline.

I knocked on the door frame again; and she ushered me into her office.

"Sister, Deb Bennett is really fading fast."

"I know," she said softly in a compassionate tone. "She's almost ready to leave us."

"So would it be appropriate, you think, for me to encourage her to let go?"

"Remember," she said, "Deb's job now is to die. We can't hold her back. We need to make her passing as easy as possible."

"It won't be long now, will it?" I asked.

"No, unfortunately," she answered. "She'll be alright. Just assure her that she is loved. And then release her. Tell her that it's alright."

When I returned to Deb, I noticed that the late afternoon sunlight from the outside windows had cast a ray of soft light on Deb's bed again.

"Deb," I said, "the light shines brightly on you. Can you feel its warmth? Can you feel the energy of the light? Let's try something, okay? Do a little meditation with me."

I asked her to close her eyes and just focus on the light on her.

"Just focus on the light. Can you see it?" I asked.

She smiled faintly.

"Try to feel it," I continued. "Can you feel its warmth? Can you feel the glow?"

She continued to smile.

"Inside your mind's eye now, can you see the brightness of the light?" I asked. "See the light everywhere inside you. You are bathed in light,
214

covered in light. There is light all around you and inside you."

She seemed to enjoy the exercise. Her eyes remained tightly shut; and I could see that she was focused.

"Doesn't it feel good?" I asked. "Doesn't it feel right?"

Her expression hadn't changed.

"We will start some exercises, easy meditations, that you can do here," I told her. "You can live in the light. You can move in the light. The light will embrace you and transform you."

I told her to open her eyes.

"I'll bring Wizard tomorrow," I promised.

Back home, I started to think about Wizard. He seemed to recognize that Deb was dying, judging from his first visit to her bedside. I figured that Wizard would need some closure of his own. He would need to see that Deb was resting easy but had reached the end. Wizard needed to say goodbye.

I looked for the cat but could not find him immediately. I looked in the place he always occupied at night – Deb's old bedroom.

The room was now devoid of furniture and bare, but the outline of her old furniture remained pressed into the green carpet. And that's where I found Wizard – curled up inside the outline of where Deb's bed had been. Following the outline of her bed, I could see that Wizard had resumed his old spot where the foot of Deb's bed had been. Yes, Wizard missed Deb.

The next night after work, I told Wizard that Deb wanted to see him one last time. I asked him if he wanted to see Deb. I opened the cat carrier in front of him; and he willingly walked straight into the carrier without any further prompting. He was ready.

At the hospice·center, I opened up the cat carrier at the foot of Deb's bed, as before. The bed seemed bigger than the last time I'd placed Wizard's crate there, as Deb's physical presence was getting smaller and smaller in the narrow frame.

Wizard slowly and methodically walked across Deb's reclining body until he found a comfortable place for the two of them atop her chest. He just sat there quietly and still, looking into her eyes with complete devotion.

Deb had little recognition of her cat on this visit, however. When I told her that Wizard had come to visit her again, she swiveled her eyes toward him, without moving her body. Their eyes met for a moment, as they connected.

Wizard continued to sit there on her chest like that for a few quiet minutes. Then he got back into his carrier.

216

Back home, the cat seemed to recognize that his association had drawn to an end, as he spent the night in my bedroom and not in Deb's old bedroom, as before. I did keep the cat flap open as a doorway for Wizard to visit her room, however. Frankly, I didn't have enough extra hours in the day after work, home maintenance, landlord responsibilities, and visiting Deb to spend much time looking after her cat or mine, either, at that critical time. I fed him, kept his water fresh, changed his personal litter box, and brushed him occasionally. But Wizard was pretty much on his own.

My next visit with Deb marked a change in tactics. In my own mind, I thought of it as a "come to Jesus moment," as much for me as for Deb. It was time to face the reality of the situation and ready ourselves for the inevitable outcome.

I just looked into her eyes for a while and got her to look into my eyes. That seemed hard for her to do.

"You have been so very brave," I told her. "You have fought the good fight. You are holding on, holding back. And everyone is so proud of you. You are a remarkable person.

"But maybe it's time now to stop fighting. It's only your body that has worn out, you know. Inside, you are very alive and healthy. You are vibrant and filled with light. That will not change. That will never change. The real you that lives inside that tired body will live forever. You know that, right? When you close your eyes to sleep, you continue to see. You sleep, yet you are aware. The light inside you continues to shine. That light can never be extinguished. You know that, right? "

Her eyes seemed to brighten. Her drawn face seemed to soften, releasing some of the tension that had gripped her so long.

"Remember Star Trek?" I asked her. "Those people could go anywhere in the blink of an eye. They could materialize anywhere. They had harnessed the energy – the natural energy, all around them and inside them. They moved freely and instantly through the stars.

"You are just like those people," I said. "Death has no hold on you. All that has worn out is your physical body. That's all. Think of the crab that outgrows his shell and moves on to another place. It's just his outer shell that he outlived. Think about the butterfly that emerges from the old body of a caterpillar. The caterpillar does not die but is transformed into a beautiful butterfly that soars freely through the endless sky. Or think of the snake that sheds his outer skin. He gets another. It's time for them to move on, to grow. They do not hold on, clinging to their old, worn out physical body. They bravely move on.

"It's okay for you to move on, too. It's okay for you to abandon this tired, old body. It's okay to let go to move forward. That is a brave thing to do.

218

"All of us will miss you dearly. But you will always be in our hearts and in our memories. And we will be in yours. And we will meet again."

A sort of graceful calm seemed to come over Deb's face. There had been a tightness in her face, as she seemed to be fighting to hang onto life. The tightness, however, seemed to be fading daily. It was difficult to tell how she really felt about what I had said, as she could not speak. But she did appear calmer.

It occurred to me that she might have been holding on and fighting to stay alive there to satisfy her friends and family. After all, we had urged her to fight. Why? As the good Sister had told me in her office when Deb first arrived at the hospice center, Deb's job there was to die.

I said goodbye for now to Deb to head into the office. I wanted to touch base with the head nurse again. She was the one who best understood the circumstance that the rest of us had refused to immediately grasp.

This time I just walked into the office and sat down in the guest chair. I didn't speak at first. Then I greeted the nun in charge.

"I am encouraging Deb to let go and stop fighting. I should have done it long ago. All of her friends, I guess, are starting to do this now, too. We want her passing to be as peaceful and gentle as possible, not having her fighting all the way."

"That's good," she said. "It will be over soon. Deb will be at peace soon. It's been a hard road. But it's coming to an end. We need to make her passing as easy as possible."

I thanked her for everything she had done for Deb and the care she continued to provide.

"There is something that you can help me with now," she said. "I need to give Deb an important shot. I could use your help, if you are willing to help me with that."

I told her that I would help any way I could and rose quickly to my feet. Once I stood up, however, I wondered why another nurse was not asked to assist her. There were simply too many patients there, I reasoned. It was plausible that the staff found themselves short-handed on occasion. And I was glad to help.

She said that she would meet me at Deb's bedside shortly. When we met at Deb's bed, I noticed that the nun held a large needle in one hand. She held it to one side, so that it would not appear alarming.

"Just hold Deb in place while I give her this shot," she told me. "We don't want her to move at all. This is a very important shot for Deb, and I want it to go smoothly. Okay?" she asked.

I just nodded my head and positioned myself to hold Deb's arms in place. I didn't anticipate that

Deb would move, but I wanted to have my hands in a position to hold her fast, just in case.

The nun focused intently on the task at hand. It was just a shot, but she appeared determined that this shot would go well. It seemed especially important to her.

It took a while once the needle had penetrated Deb's body for all of the contents in the shot to be distributed. The nun leaned over to make certain that the contents were expelled before extracting the needle. She held the large shot gun carefully at her side again. Then she patted Deb gently on her forehead.

"Thank you," she told me. "Deb will rest easily now."

After she had left Deb's bedside, I wondered whether this injection would be Deb's last shot. I wondered what was in the needle. Would this nun who viewed herself as first and foremost a nurse actually give Deb a shot to end all of her physical suffering?

I stayed with Deb for a while to determine the outcome of the shot. Soon she was sleeping peacefully, but she was still physically alive.

I drove home to get some rest before my next visit.

Chapter 12
Mid-January 1993

Deb's birthday had come and gone without any notice. To my knowledge, nobody celebrated, or even wished her a happy birthday. I wouldn't even have thought about it, except that I ran across her rental application when I was reviewing leases. She was only 33 years old.

She completed her six-month lease period when she went into the hospital in the fall. Altogether, I had known Deb for less than a year, yet our lives seemed intertwined. Yes, she was just my renter; and yet I felt responsible for her. How could I not have detected the severity of her condition much earlier when she complained of a never-ending cold without any coughing or sneezing? How could I fail to recognize the significance of her several slips on the stairs and her dwindling energy on the many days I had observed her at our Victorian home? If Deb was in denial that her brain tumor could have returned after such a long and celebrated remission, then so was I.

Recognizing that my visiting time with Deb would now be short, I settled on a plan to make the most of every short trip to her bedside. She had grown weak and could not focus or stay awake very long during these visits.

Deb would leave us soon; and I wanted to help make her passing easier if possible, so that she left without a struggle and moved forward with clarity. I wanted to help her get to the other side without fear, confusion, or apprehension. I wanted her to die with grace, walking willingly forward.

What awaited her? That's probably what everyone who faces death wonders on some level, regardless of their convictions and how they have lived their lives. Could Deb be prepared for death? That gave me a series of ideas. It was time to prepare Deb for the transition ahead of her, to walk her to the doorway and help her open the door.

So many people die reluctant to leave this world behind or afraid to leave. This is no doubt the problem with ghosts, people who are reluctant, afraid, or simply too confused to leave this physical world behind. I had seen and heard ghosts. I'd even received training to help people deal with ghosts who haunted their homes by helping the dead recognize their condition and encouraging them to move on fully.

We will all die and leave behind our mortal coil. Death is just a fact of life. But death is no end. It's a time of transition from this world to the next. Nobody really dies; we just graduate from one world to another. How can the eternal life force inside us end? It is pure energy. We see it most obviously in the electromagnetic energy that lives within us and surrounds us everywhere we go. It is our pure consciousness that exists outside and independent of the physical body. It is our divine spark and cannot be extinguished. We are immortal. It's only our physical body that dies – the outer wrapping of the inner self.

The ancients knew that. *The Tibetan Book of the Dead* suggests how people need to prepare themselves for the maze they will encounter at the time of physical death. It can be confusing on many levels with potentially many distractions. Everyone can negotiate their way through the light and find their way. But emotional and mental impulses can grab at you and pull you away from the light. Voices may call to you to lure you away. And all of that happens shortly after your physical life expires and you find yourself wandering outside the body, trying to find a place you have never been before. The transition should be natural for everyone but is not necessarily easy.

I wanted this transition to be easy and natural for Deb. All of her friends and family wanted that. But the moment of surrender was fast approaching. Would she be ready?

At the hospice center, I pulled up a chair to Deb's bed. I moved close to her and took one of her hands into mine. Slowly, she opened her eyes without much expression.

"Let's do something, okay?" I asked. "Remember when you closed your eyes and felt the light inside you? Let's do that again. Only this time, it will be even better. It will be just as good as a ride through the stars on the USS Enterprise. It will be just like Star-Trek."

Her eyes widened, and it seemed to me that a small smile was forming.

"Just close your eyes," I said, "Tune out everything outside yourself. All you will hear is my voice. Go deep within yourself. Keep going deeper and deeper until you find the center of your very soul. That's the real you. That's where you really live.

"You see nothing. You hear nothing. All that you see now is a blank screen in front of you. Do you see it? It's a clear, blank screen.

"Now fill the screen with light. Let the light that is all around you and inside you fill the screen. You see nothing but light. You see it with your mind's eye. There is light everywhere. You are filled with light.

"The light is warm and glows. It is electric and alive. You are standing in the light. Do you feel it? Can you feel its warm glow?

"Just focus on the light and feel the power and potential of the light inside you."

She held my hand a little tighter; and I noticed that her hand was hot. A satisfied look fell upon her face; and she began to relax a little.

"Stay in the light," I told her. "You can live in the light. You can move in the light. The light can take you anywhere. The light is pure – pure energy. The light holds you in its embrace."

We just remained like that for some time. Deb kept her eyes closed. She looked at peace. I gently retracted my hand from hers and cupped it on her forehead. Then I slowly brushed her long, blond hair from her face.

She remained in this tranquil state, so I rose to take my chair away and place it where I had originally found it. None of the beds seemed to have their own guest chairs. Many items in the large room where Deb was stationed with so many others floated here and there without a fixed place. All of the parts were interchangeable. Everyone and everything here was pretty much the same.

Repositioning the chair, I scanned the room and the adjacent hallway where various nuns were moving quietly and efficiently about their nursing duties. There was little interaction among staff or between staff and patients. The place was always deadly quiet, with these angels of mercy slipping almost unnoticed among the many beds.

When I returned home the next night after work, I lay on my back in my bedroom after changing clothes to visit Deb again. I wondered how I could continue to help her make this life-changing transition. Like the rest of her friends, I was torn inside by a sense of failure to really restore her physical health in time and the sense that I would soon need to say goodbye to her. I had been careful not to say goodbye after recent visits with the realistic fear that I would never see her again.

On my back, I closed my eyes and tried to see the light inside my own mind's eye, as I had directed Deb to do. Yes, it worked very well. The light was warm and embracing. I could feel its energy and potential. There was much that this light could do for Deb. I conditioned myself for the work ahead of us, with more exercises to take Deb where she needed to go.

When I arrived later at the hospice center, the night air was cold with swirling snow flurries. The world seemed so desolate that I had to remind myself once again that winter was only a time when nature slumbers to ready itself for the bright spring days ahead. There is always light, although it is not always obvious to the eye. Artificial lights from the holiday season to usher in the new year still adorned the entry to the hospice. People put out these lights every year at the darkest time of the year to remind us of the promise of the return of brighter days. I thought about the nuns hanging these lights in the reception area. I hadn't really noticed the holiday lights much before. Now that the holidays were over, they stuck out.

Someone must have recently visited Deb, because a guest chair remained at her bedside. I wondered if she could handle so many guests and then remembered how precious her remaining time with all of us was.

Her eyes were open when I sat down next to her, and she looked directly into my face. There was an alertness here that I'd seldom seen during her hospice stay. Perhaps she was eager to see me and continue our exercises. Was she eager to return to the light?

"You look wide awake," I told her. "I see you've had plenty of visitors today. A lot of people love you."

She smiled weakly.

"Are you ready for more exercises? Are you ready for the light?"

As always, she remained speechless. Her inability to put words together was something we had seen for many long weeks now. She was probably too weak speak, even if she could.

I pulled my chair as close to her as possible and lay one hand upon her nearest forearm.

"Just close your eyes," I suggested. "You are going to like this, I promise. Close your eyes but stay very alert.

"Clear your mind of any thoughts and tune out all external sounds and distractions. Go deeper and deeper. Go all the way to the center of your being. When you get there, you'll feel the eternal peace and bliss that is your very soul.

"And now you see the light inside you. Just focus your mind's eye on the light. This is the light from all around you and inside you. It shines forever. It cannot be destroyed. It cannot be removed. Do you see it? Do you see the light?

"Now focus your attention on that light and focus your full force of your will. Make the light grow ever brighter. Focus your intent. There is just you and the light. And together you form a little dance. See how the light bounces? Make the light even brighter.

"Now there is light all around you and inside you. You are engulfed in the light. The light can take you anywhere. It is the ultimate power. And you and the light are one.

"You are standing in the light. You are living in the light. Can you feel it?"

Deb's face softened with a grace that told me she felt the light. I rubbed her arm gently.

"When it feels right to you," I said, "you can open your eyes again. You can stay in the light longer, too, if you want. It's totally up to you."

Deb's eyes remained closed, but I could see that she was alert and enjoying the experience.

"I will leave you then for a little while," I said, "but I will be back. We will continue working with the light. More tomorrow, okay?"

Back home the next day, a Saturday, I found myself meditating on my back on my bed again. I wanted to see exactly what Deb saw. I saw the light exactly as she had seen. The task now was to make this an even more active exercise. I wanted to show Deb how to move in the light.

I drove the two or three miles from our Victorian house to the hospice center and got there late in the late afternoon.

I slipped beside Deb again. She looked ready for me and ready to continue.

"Deb," I said, "you don't need me to help you see the light. You can do it totally on your own. The light is always there for you. You just have to want it."

The intense afternoon sunlight from the window cast itself upon her bed. I pointed this out to Deb and asked if she could turn her head toward the sunlight. She tried to move her head. I readjusted her head on the pillow to help her make this slight change that seemed so difficult for her to do on her own.

"Today we'll see how you can control the light," I said. "It's easy, really - when you have done it once or twice.

"Just close your eyes and stay alert. You need your deeper awareness for this. You will not see with your eyes or hear with your ears. You don't need them. You have something much better.

"Focus only on the light. Do you see the light? Can you make it glow brighter and make it bounce?"

It was obvious to me that she was trying. She was trying very hard.

"This is nothing that should come hard," I said. "It should come easy. "Keep your eyes closed, but flutter your eyelids a little, to let a little light from outside filter through your eyelashes. Just flutter your eyelashes a little, as you let the light come inside you. Let more light come into you.

"As you do this, notice how the light bounces with energy. Now focus your attention on the light. Make the light turn yellow. Focus your attention on the light with the full power of your will. Make the light turn yellow, so all that you see now is yellow light. Can you see it?"

The strain left her face, replaced by a look of content.

"Good," I said. "Now make the light turn orange. Focus your attention on the light and make it turn orange. Now all you see is orange light. See how it bounces with energy?"

Her facial expression told me that all was going well. She was a ready student.

"Now make the light turn reddish blue. Focus. Make the light glow reddish blue. Do you see it? Good. Now make the light orange again. It's a pure, bright orange. You see this orange light deep within you. Feel the different energy of the orange light. Now make the light yellow again. Focus on the light and make it yellow. A warm, yellow light fills you up. You see the yellow everywhere. You see vast fields of yellow. Good. You are doing very well. You are becoming one with the light; and the energy can take you anywhere. You can move instantly anywhere you want to go, riding on a wave of the light. The light goes beyond time and space."

I encouraged her to open her eyes again, if that felt right to her. She did so, and I concluded that the exercise had been very fulfilling.

"You can manifest and project light and transform it, too," I told her. "You can move freely in the light. You can do all of that with your consciousness. It has nothing to do with your body. Isn't that wonderful?!" I said. "Isn't that liberating? You are free! Nothing can hold you back."

She was going to be alright, I told myself. Deb was going to make it out of here okay. I squeezed her hand, kissed her forehead, and left.

Meditating on my back in bed the next day, I realized that we needed to speed up the exercises. These exercises had been inspired by things that I had read, studied and heard about, but were tailored now for Deb's condition pretty much on the spot. Deb was growing weak, but we had more work to do with light before she left us. I recognized that we would need to focus on walking Deb through the next steps. I had an idea where these steps would lead us, but it was not easy to go there. These next steps might see Deb walk out of the hospice alive and strong after all – not in a physical body, but in an energy body fully charged.

The urgency of getting Deb ready and taking her through all of the light exercises in time got the best of me. I rushed out the front door and slipped on front steps that I had failed to shovel. Yes, I was getting behind on things at home and at work. Deb's final days were taking a toll on me emotionally and eating into my time and physical energy.

Now was not the time to think about any of that, however. Deb's deterioration physically was the only reality I could face. I'm certain that her other friends and family felt the same way. All I had to give Deb now were these exercises. I had to believe that they would help.

There were few cars in the hospice parking lot that night. A lot of people have trouble saying goodbye, especially when the terminally ill are not responsive at the end.

Deb was different. She could go inside her and find an inner strength and direction. She had quickly learned how to absorb, process, and transform light. In a couple more days, she could become a master. Did we have a couple more days?

"Hey, I'm back," I said. "Have you been practicing? Have you been looking for the light?"

She motioned with one cupped hand for me to sit down. It was more motion that I'd seen from her in some time.

"Today, we're going to move in the light. You have seen how you can go deep inside yourself and find the light. You have stood in the light and made it glow. But today we will see that you can move in the light. Are you ready?"

She closed her eyes instantly. But it wasn't because she wanted to sleep. I could see that she was alert and eager to begin.

"You are standing in the light. Can you see the light all around you? You are bathed in the light. It is warm and bright. It embraces you. It empowers you. Feel its energy. You are one with the light."

I looked at her face to see if she was there. That calm grace I had seen before with earlier exercises was back. She was there.

"That's good. That's good. You're doing fine. Today we're going to see how you can move in the light. The light will always be with you. It can take you anywhere. It can take you out of this room, out of this body, out of this world. You don't need your eyes. You don't need your ears. You don't need your legs or your heart or any of that. Your consciousness merges with the light. Your consciousness is the light. Let your consciousness, your pure energy and life force, merge with the eternal light. Are you ready?"

She was breathing calmly, as though it was going well. She was focused and taking it all in.

"You are standing in the bright light. In front of you now you see a door. Go ahead and open that door. Don't be afraid. The light will always be with you. It's important that you open the door."

Watching her carefully, I could tell that she was balking at this next step. Opening the door was scary. When you bask in the comfort of light, it's hard to take a daring step into the unknown.

"Don't worry," I told her. "There's nothing on the other side of that door to frighten you. It's just something new. There's nothing wrong with something new. It just represents change. Everything changes. Things that don't change simply stagnate. They do not move. They do not

235

grow. They do not continue. Trust the light. The light will always be with you. Just reach out and open the door...."

I closed my own eyes and took one of her hands. I entered the light with her, bringing the light into my own consciousness, deep inside me. In my mind's eye, through the light, I saw her standing there. She was hunched over, staring at the door.

"It's okay," I said. "I wouldn't take you anywhere bad, anywhere dangerous. Trust the light."

She took a deep breath and then exhaled, with a sigh of relief. She had gone beyond the door.

"It's okay that it seems strange to you there. Maybe it seems dark at first. Focus on bringing back the light. There is always light. You are the light. Fill that dark room with the light. Do you see the room beginning to fill now with light?

"You are safe in this place," I told her. "The light surrounds you. Now you can feel yourself in this new place. And it is good.

"Now look ahead of you. There is another door. Don't be afraid of this new door. You have gone through one door. You can go through another. Move forward in the light. Open the new door. Walk inside. It seems dark at first. Then the light returns. And you feel yourself in that room. It's good. You are moving forward. Can you feel yourself in this room? Do you feel that you belong there?"

To my surprise, Deb grunted softly. It was a good sign.

"You can open any door and walk through that door. It might seem dark at first, but your light will fill the room. And you will be at home there. Life is just like opening doors. We open one door, and then we open another. Life is eternal, with many doors. Light is eternal. You are eternal."

I squeezed her hand and then stood up. I lay one palm on her forehead. She smiled, with eyes still closed.

"You can come and go any time you want now," I told her. "Just open the door and fill it with light."

On my drive home from the hospice, I had a lot to think about. Deb was fading fast physically. But she was also progressing fast on another level. I might have only one more exercise with her. I wondered how to make the most of it.

In *The Tibetan Book of the Dead*, people are conditioned to negotiate their way through a transitional phase called death. It is assumed that there is no absolute death in the sense that everything comes to an end. The spirit of persons who face physical death is taxed with the task of negotiating their way through a maze of confusing twists and turns. They encounter distractions that attempt to lure them away from a proper course of safe passage from this transitory world to a life beyond the physical plane. It's a tough transition for people who are not properly conditioned and aware, as they stumble through the maze. Transformation is not easy.

Deb was not an ancient Tibetan. But her journey ahead could be just that frightening. I wanted to give her confidence, direction, and light to take with her. I know that we can move in the light.

By the next night, I had a plan. Before leaving the house, I lay on my back and worked myself through the very exercise that I had in mind for Deb. I knew it could work. It would give her everything she needed to walk between the worlds when she took her last breath. She wouldn't need to breathe. Her consciousness could live outside her physical body. With it, she could move in the light. She would be ready.

I moved beside her quickly and tried to determine whether she was ready for the next phase in our exercises. She was very weak but did look eager to begin.

"Are you ready to move in the light tonight?" I asked her. "I've saved the very best for tonight. You're going to like this, I promise you."

She fumbled to find my hand. I reached out to grab it. I remained standing beside her bed.

"Close your eyes and see the light. All that you see is the light. It is very bright and energetic. It is warm and inviting. Now you see the door in front of you. You have opened this door before and gone inside. It's easy. The door is waiting for you, like an old friend that welcomes you. Just open the door.

"You are now inside the next room. The light fills that room, too. You fill the room. The room welcomes you. Focus on the light. Make it glow brighter and bounce with energy. You merge with the light. You control the light. You are one with the light.

"Now make the light turn yellow. The yellow is becoming more and more intense. It is a beautiful, overpowering yellow. Isn't this wonderful? You are welcome here.

"You see another door in front of you. It's much like the other door. Just reach out and grab it. Everything will be okay. When you pass through the door, it will be even more wonderful.

"You are now in the other room. There is light here also. You feel at home here. Your presence fills the room. Do you see the light? Does it feel good?"

"Uh-huh," Deb muttered. It was more than she had articulated in some time. She was very focused.

"Good. Now make this light turn orange. Just focus your attention on the light and make it turn orange. See it turning orange now? The orange is soft at first, and then it grows more intense. Now it's a fiery, vibrant orange. The whole room glows with this orange light. And you are one with the light.

"There is another door in front of you. Every door is a new adventure, a new beginning. You are moving in the light. Reach out and open that door. And now move inside that room.

"As before, this room is filled with your light. It is warming and inviting. Your presence fills the room. Now focus your attention on the light in this new room. Make it glow a reddish blue. It is the most beautiful shade of reddish blue light. And the light fills the room and electrifies the room. And you feel the energy there. You are riding on the waves of this light, moving freely.

"And now you see another door in front of you. It's another great opportunity to discover and explore your new freedom. Open this door. Light fills this room, too. You are one with the light. You control the light. What color is the light? Can you see it?"

Deb's face showed a high level of intense concentration.

"Is the light blue in this room?" I asked. "Can you make the room blue with light? The blue light appears very soft at first, almost a pastel blue. As you focus your attention on it, the light intensifies and becomes darker and bolder. Now the room is blue as the ocean. The room is blue as the sky on a beautiful day. And the blue light is soothing and calming. It holds you in its embrace. There is blue light above you, on all sides, and below you. You are bathed in blue light. And you are safe and warm and strong there. You are one with the light. You have merged with the light."

I looked quickly at Deb's face. An expression of calm and serenity had come over her. There was no disguising her feelings at this stage of her physical illness. She had no brave masks left or the energy to wear them. I could look into her face and know exactly how she felt about things. And she looked content and at peace.

"That's good, Deb," I told her. "You have done very well. You are going to be okay now. You can stay in the light as long as you like and travel there freely. "

I patted her gently on the forehead and took one long look at my friend.

From her bedside, I walked to the office. The head nurse was busy at her desk. I could tell from her posture that it had been a long day for her. I knocked on the side of her door frame; and she motioned for me to come inside and sit.

"I've just spent some time with Deb," I told her. "She's going to be okay. Deb's ready now."

The nun stood up. She smiled.

"That's good," she said. "It's good that she's ready now. "She's suffered long enough."

My drive home was filled with memories of my friend. I knew that she would not be with us much longer. But I was happy that she had reached a place where she felt comfortable about leaving. Maybe we could practice moving in the light a few more times. I hoped so. On the other hand, Deb had suffered in her decaying body long enough. It was time for her to move on. The good sister knew that. Now Deb's friends were on board, too. Deb seemed ready.

Chapter 13
Late January 1993

I lay on my bed the next night trying to work myself up for another exercise with Deb. I wondered whether I should walk her through the steps again, opening new door after new door so she could feel the welcoming light. Was there anything else that I could do to make her feel empowered and comfortable to leave her broken, physical body behind?

Focused deeply on Deb, I felt a connection to her that was very strong. I closed my eyes and held my attention on her. I expected to see a plan of action forming in my mind's eye. I thought that I might visualize how I could work out another exercise with Deb at her bedside. I wanted to visualize what we might do next, so that it was clear to me how things would go. I knew that she was at the end.

To my surprise, Deb appeared very clearly in my mind's eye – only she was wearing her white hospice bathrobe and tip-toeing down stairs. Even more odd, she was walking down the stairs from her third-floor bedroom in our Victorian house. Despite being dressed in her hospice gown, she stood fairly erect and walked nimbly down the stairs. She was moving quickly and cautiously, as though with great stealth.

Fascinated by my vision, I continued to watch the image inside my mind's eye. I was very cognizant that I was awake and not dreaming. I remained in a heightened state of consciousness, meditating on my back in bed. My eyes were closed. It was like watching an engrossing motion picture inside my head.

At the bottom of the stairs, Deb rested her right hand on the railing post, as she slid around to the right of the staircase. She walked across the parquet floor in the dining room and through the opening to the next room. Now she was in the living room where she had spent so many days seated on her wicker rocker watching Star-Trek on television. She moved with purpose across the room to the round wicker basket that held the cat toys. She squatted down in her bathrobe beside the basket and scanned the contents, as though looking for something in particular.

Wizard the cat entered the picture, approaching Deb by the basket. She reached out with her left hand to pet the cat. Wizard sat down there on the green carpet beside Deb.

Then Deb sat down on the green carpet and continued to pet her black cat. He sat very still for her.

While resting her left hand on the cat, Deb peered into the wicker basket and then began to paw through the contents with her other hand. At last, she lifted something out of the basket. Her hand rose higher and higher above the basket, as she retrieved the long item.

I focused harder to determine what she was lifting from the basket; and then the image became clearer. Deb held a long pink ribbon. It was delicate and twirled above her.

She dangled the pink ribbon above the cat. Deb was playing with her cat. Old Mr. Wizard swatted the ribbon and then tried to pin it between both front paws. I continued to watch Deb and her cat play with the ribbon. It occurred to me that I had never seen that ribbon in the wicker basket before.

In fact, I had never seen Deb with that pink ribbon before.

She dangled it above the cat some more and then returned the ribbon to the basket. She held the ribbon high above the basket before dropping it. The ribbon fluttered a little, as it slowly descended into the basket. I watched as the last of the pink ribbon disappeared into the wicker basket.

A ringing telephone disrupted my vision. It was hard to clear my head to stand up. I ran down the third-floor steps to the wall phone in the kitchen. I felt disoriented but tried to answer the phone coherently.

"Hello," was the best I could manage. I must have sounded a million miles away.

It was Sandra. Her voice was very soft and weak.

"Were you coming in tonight?" she asked. "To the hospice."

I answered yes, but that I wasn't quite ready.

"Good," she said. "I'll see you when you get here then."

"What is it?" I asked.

"Deb died today," she said. "Just a little while ago."

"Strange," I said, remembering my vision of Deb returning to the house to play with the cat.

"Huh?" Sandra said.

"Okay," I said. "I'll be there right away."

"Her parents are already here," Sandra said. "And Anita, too."

"Anything you want me to do?" I asked.

"No, just get here soon, okay?"

I returned to my bedroom and got ready to go. Still dazed, I wandered into the kitchen and drank milk from the carton. I went to the coat closet and put on my winter coat, scarf, and hat. It was a cold winter day outside. It was not the kind of day anyone would choose to die. I felt badly that Deb had not made it to the spring, so I could take her on another trip somewhere outdoors.

I headed to the front door to leave, but then felt a strange compulsion to go look inside Deb's wicker basket in the living room. Wizard the cat was sitting near the basket. I pet the cat and then looked into the basket. On top of all of the cat toys was a large pink ribbon. I had never seen it there before. I had only seen it in my vision of Deb minutes ago. It occurred to me that Deb had died before she appeared in my vision. Eerie, I thought. Like a ghost. But where had the ribbon come from?

At the hospice center, Sandra, Anita, and Deb's parents were gathered outside a large white enclosure. White screen panels wrapped around Deb's bed like a private tent.

Nobody was talking or doing much. Deb's parents were whispering to each other a few feet away from Deb's girlfriends. Anita and Sandra awkwardly looked down at the ground. It was an odd moment, when all time and motion seemed to stand still.

I noticed that the nurses continued to make their rounds, keeping a distance from Deb's enclosed bed and her visitors. When the head nurse walked near us, I moved forward to speak with her. I kept my voice low.

"Sister, excuse me," I said.

She turned to give me her undivided attention. Her expression had not changed from the day I first met her.

"What happens next?" I asked. "I mean ... what about the coroner, removing the body, notice of death to the newspaper."

"We'll take care of all that," the nun said. "Everything will be handled here."

I thanked her and returned to the parents and friends of Deb, still standing outside the tent that held her remains.

"How does she look?" I asked Sandra. "Did she look peaceful and calm at the end?"

She nodded yes.

I asked whether she had spent some time with the body. Again, she nodded yes.

"I looked forward to going to We Fest with Deb again this summer," Anita said. "We did that every year. We missed this last summer, though. Deb said she was busy at home. You know, that was my big connection to Deb. We Fest will not be the same. I probably won't go again."

I told her that Deb would want her to go and that she could go for both of them. Anita continued to stare at the floor.

"I want to say goodbye to Deb," I said. "Is that okay?"

Sandra said it was okay. She said Deb would like that.

I slid around one of the white screen panels that guarded her bed. Deb was reclining on her back with arms to the side, as usual. But a serene look of surrender now filled her face. She looked noble, as though she had reached some plateau.

I noticed that she wore the same white hospice bathrobe that I had seen in my vision just before coming to the hospice center.

All of the life was gone from her face. Her look was vacant. I knew that she was gone. I assumed that she had walked through the many doors of light and found each new room to be bright and welcoming. She had left us without fear or hesitancy. She was ready. I had to believe that. The expression on her face seemed to bear that out.

I leaned over to whisper in her ear.

"You are safe now," I told her. "You are beyond pain and worry. You are free as the air and filled with light. Everywhere you go, you will be at home and welcome. I am so very proud of you. You have been so brave."

I kissed her one last time on the forehead and then brushed the long blond hair from her eyes. Someone had already closed her eyes for her. She no longer needed them. She had a greater vision now.

"We will all remember you and your little quirks. We will hold you in our hearts forever and always love you. And we will all be together again."

I wondered if she could hear me wherever her consciousness now resided. I did not sense her presence there. I wondered what she might want to hear me say.

"Your cat Wizard will be safe and have a good life with me. He will live in our Victorian house with your things."

I took one long last look at her and remarked again how tall and elegant she looked. But that was the shell she had discarded. The real Deb was far, far away.

"Goodbye," I said.

Outside the screened enclosure again, I walked up to Deb's mother. Her father had left the room.

"I'm so sorry for your loss," I told her. "Is there anything I can do?"

"We will take care of all of the arrangements. We'll let you know when the service is."

I sat down in a chair near them. I wanted to remain with them for support but felt that I needed a little space for myself for a few minutes. Deb's journey was over. She had left us. And she was only 33 years old.

Somewhere in the building, a phone kept ringing. I wondered why one of the nurses did not answer it. Then I remembered how busy they were with so many patients.

At last, the ringing stopped. The whole building suddenly seemed so quiet. It was a vacant feeling, emptiness. Maybe it was always that way at the hospice center. I hadn't really noticed it before.

People here were always dying. Several people had probably died during the time I had been visiting Deb, but I had not noticed.

One of the nuns, one I did not know well, walked up to me and bent over to speak to me privately.

"Someone on the phone is calling for your friend Deb," she said. "I tried to explain the situation to him, but he would not listen. He says he was her landlord. I thought that you were her landlord. Could you please speak with him?"

How strange, I thought. Who would be calling Deb here, of all places. I rose from the chair and followed the nurse to the office phone. She handed me the receiver.

I introduced myself as Deb's friend and landlord.

"Well, I want to speak to Deb," he said in a gruff voice. "See, she cheated me out of some rent. It's taken me awhile, but I took it to court. She didn't show, so I won. The court ruled in my favor. She and her roommate left owing me money. They turned me into the city on a lot of trumped up charges and got me into a lot of trouble. But I cleared all that up, and now Deb owes me money. She owes me for the rent she withheld. I couldn't find the other girl, but I got a judgment against Deb. You tell her. There's a court judgment against her, and she has to pay."

Now I had this guy pegged. This was the landlord that Deb had left before coming to live with me. It seemed like a million years ago, but it was less than a year ago really. This was the landlord that Deb had turned into the city for violations. She had withheld rent during the time the violations were not addressed. And now this guy had taken her to court when she could not defend herself and probably gotten a small claims court judgment against her, because she had failed to appear. I didn't know whether to laugh or cry.

"Well, it seems that the last laugh is on you then, mister," I said. "Deb didn't appear because she was dying in a hospice center. You have tracked her down to the hospice center. I'm here with her friends. You see, Deb died today. So, you are not getting one thin dime."

I hung up the phone.

Sandra asked what the phone call was about. I told her, and she just shook her head from side to side.

"Unbelievable," she said. "All that poor girl went through. And then that guy calls like that. To think

252

that someone would track her down in a hospice."

"Well, she's rid of him now. Rid of all this mess. She'll be fine. Really."

Anita gave me an odd look.

"Call me if you hear anything about a memorial service, viewing times, or the burial," I asked Sandra.

"Oh, we're going to try to have her cremated," she said.

"Yes," Anita added, "so we can spread her ashes over the campgrounds at We Fest."

I turned to leave, looking from side to side throughout the building one last time. I would never be here again. None of us would.

Driving home, I wondered whether Deb could be cremated or whether she would be buried now in a church cemetery. Well, it didn't really matter. The real Deb, her essential life force, had walked through the light. What happened to her decaying body at this point was rather meaningless.

I couldn't sleep when I got home. The sudden news that Deb had died still wore on me, as did seeing her body in repose and getting that nasty phone call in the middle of everything.

Wizard was still in the living room next to the wicker basket. I looked again at the mysterious pink ribbon that had materialized out of nowhere. Had Deb really visited the house one last time and played with her beloved cat once more before departing?

I wondered where Deb had found the pink ribbon. In my vision, she had carried it down the stairs, as though coming from her room. At the other end of the third-floor landing was my bedroom.

I couldn't help inspecting her empty bedroom to look around. Had I missed anything when I looked there before? It seemed that her parents had pretty much taken everything from the room except for the table that had been her kitchen table before moving. I looked again into the closet that once held her long row of red Lancôme Paris blazers for the cosmetic counter at Dayton's department store. The closet was now empty. I even opened the little door to the old attic crawl space, a remnant of the 1970's remodeling that converted most of the third floor from rafters to bedrooms and bathroom. There was nothing in the crawl space but insulation and wooden beams.

Leaving Deb's bedroom, however, I spotted a place that I had overlooked. Between the two bedrooms was a small linen closet. It was actually closer to Deb's bedroom and the third-floor bathroom than my bedroom. I couldn't remember just then whether I had put much of anything into that little closet. Had Deb?

Opening the linen closet, I found an extra pillow, blankets, sheets, some concrete blocks that had once been a book case, and other assorted things that someone had stashed there for storage. Lifting up the blankets and pillows, I found a shoe box filled with ribbons. They were pink ribbons, exactly like the one in Wizard's wicker basket. Next to the box of ribbons, I found a smaller box with sewing things. Beside both boxes were some ribbons that had been transformed into bows. One bow was attached to a small teddy bear.

Deb had been secretly making Christmas gifts in her bedroom. She was probably working on her craft work right up until fall when she went into the hospital. She probably envisioned that she had two and a half months left to comfortably complete her projects.

I had no idea what exactly she had planned for all of the ribbons and other sewing accessories or who should receive the projects. It was unfinished work. The scissors that she had used to cut the long, pink ribbons sat next to the shoe box, exactly where she last had positioned it a few months earlier.

I decided to keep all of the ribbons and assorted craft work exactly where Deb had hidden it. Future renters and roommates would come and go at our Victorian house, wondering what the ribbons were all about. Only Deb and I knew.

They were beautiful ribbons.

Chapter 14
January-February 1993

I thought that was the end of Deb, and that she was out of my life there at the old Victorian house that we had once shared. But there is no real end to life and no death where spirit is concerned. Her higher consciousness would continue to explore, and her eternal life force would burn brightly like the sun. Deb had learned how to move in the light.

So, it shouldn't have surprised me much when I heard from Deb again after we had left her corpse at the hospice center. And she made herself heard in a most auditory way.

I had been hanging around the house after work since Deb's passing, waiting for the phone to ring with news from Sandra or Deb's parents about a funeral or some sort of memorial service. So, my hearing was keen, as I listened for the phone to ring.

On the second day after Deb's passing, however, the silence was broken not by the sound of a phone ringing, but by the sound of a stereo playing music. I knew that I was the only person in the house at the time, so I found this music hard to fathom. I began walking through the house, trying to track the sound. After I had walked through the second floor, I walked upstairs to the third floor.

The music was coming from Deb's former bedroom.

Before I opened the door to the bedroom, my mind raced through the total evacuation of Deb's things. Her parents had taken everything out of her room. There was no stereo, TV, or radio left in that room – only her old kitchen table. I hesitated to open the door to a room that projected music, knowing there was no earthly explanation.

I bolstered my courage and opened the door. To my surprise, there was no music inside the room. The music seemed to stop as soon as I opened the door. The room was exactly the way I last saw it, empty except for Deb's kitchen table. There was no stereo or television.

Was I imagining the music inside my head? I don't think so. On the other hand, I doubt if anyone else would have heard it. The music was a message meant for me. It said that Deb had kept her word about returning to our Victorian house, if only for one last visit to her room where she had found so much comfort playing her stereo.

I closed the door to Deb's room, where the imprint of her furniture was disappearing a little more each day. Soon the imprint of her presence would not be there at all.

Downstairs, I tried to make some coffee. I looked at Deb's Proctor-Silex coffee grinder, then put it into the cupboard. I made tea instead, remembering the first day I had spoken to Deb only ten months ago.

I was listening carefully for the whistle on Deb's tea kettle. Instead, the kitchen wall phone rang. I turned off the heat to the tea kettle and moved across the room to the wall phone.

"Is this Von?" a woman asked. "This is Deb's mom," she said. "I have some details for you on Deb's service. It will be in Forest Lake, where we live. And I'd like you to be one of Deb's pallbearers."

She explained that it would be a church service with interment to follow immediately after the funeral. It was set for the weekend, as a convenience to those people who worked.

"You didn't know Deb all that long, I know, but you were important in her life," she said. "Especially at the end. You were there for her. That meant a lot to her."

After I hung up, the whole ceremony started to concern me. It would be a formal church service with a casket. Did that mean that Deb would not be cremated? And what about the cemetery burial? The idea had been to spread Deb's ashes over the campground at We Fest.

But it really didn't matter now. Deb had transcended her physical body. What the family did with the material remains was unimportant to Deb. It mattered only to the family.

Sandra called shortly after Deb's mother to make certain that I had all the details and would attend the service. She wanted me to meet with Anita and her at the church, so we could sit together. None of us really knew Deb's relatives or friends from the church or community there.

Sandra seemed surprised that I had been asked to act as one of the six pallbearers. I don't know if that was because I had known Deb such a short while or because Deb's body would be carried in a casket and not cremated. I didn't ask. I told her that I was honored just to know Deb.

That weekend, I found myself meeting with Sandra and Anita in the church parking lot. They seemed hesitant to go inside. We stood out in the parking lot in the middle of all of the cars, looking at everyone who entered the church.

One young woman wore a stylish hat, the sort that only a young woman could wear well. Anita pointed her out to me. I told her that I had no clue who that woman might be, but that it looked a little like Deb and might be a cousin or perhaps her sister.

"It's a Deb look for sure," Anita said. "Deb wore hats just like that."

Sandra agreed.

Then the two of them began comparing all of the young women who entered the church to Deb. Probably a lot of them were relatives. But maybe Sandra and Anita were trying to find a little bit of Deb alive there that day, if even for an hour or two.

Reminding them that I needed to sit with the other pallbearers, I suggested that we all go inside in a timely fashion. I found Deb's mother sitting in front with the immediate family and asked her whether she wanted me to sit in a special place. She pointed out where the pallbearers were all seated.

I told her that I would be there shortly but wanted to sit for just a minute or two with Sandra and Anita. They seemed so isolated there. The church trappings might have had something to do with it.

When I settled in with the other five pallbearers near the front of the church, I sort of lost myself in reading the program. It struck me as odd that people printed a program for a funeral. It listed various hymns that we would stand to sing as a group. There were no real remembrances of Deb that I can recall, except for the brief mentions of her in the clergyman's talk. The program gave me the impression that there would be a private interment at the cemetery maintained by the church.

Upon a signal from the priest, we six pallbearers stood as a group and filed up to the front of the church where Deb's casket sat prominently on display. We counted to pick up the casket on the count of three. It seemed light, but not empty. Deb had always been slender and had withered away over the course of four months.

Oddly, we held the casket low to the ground and did not raise it up to shoulder height. Consequently, the funeral director who had backed his hearse up to the church needed to direct us to lift the casket up to the level of the vehicle. He helped us hoist it aboard the hearse.

Once he had helped us slide the casket all the way into the back of the hearse, I asked him whether I would be needed at the cemetery. It seemed to me that the casket would need to be carried there from the hearse to the grave site.

No, he told me. That would not be necessary.

Relieved that I would not have to endure the actual burial at the church cemetery, I walked back into the church. I wondered what had happened to Sandra's plans to gather some of her ashes from cremation to sprinkle over the grounds at We Fest. Well, the family decided these matters, of course – not her friends from work.

I wandered through the church and found myself in a hallway outside the sanctuary. People were gathering up their coats there and working their way outdoors with little conversation.

A young woman who looked a lot like Deb walked up to me, as I stood against the back wall. It might have been a cousin or her younger sister.

"I am sorry for your loss," she told me.

This floored me, since apparently she was a relative; and I had known Deb for only ten months.

I just smiled and turned away without responding. I watched her walk away and decided that the hat she was wearing had been one of Deb's own hats.

The next day, I called Sandra to see how she was holding up. Our lives had revolved around visiting Deb daily for several months. Sandra said that she and Anita had not gone to the cemetery, either.

I reminded her that her plan had been to sprinkle some of Deb's ashes over the campground at the summer We Fest music festival.

"It's funny," she said, "but most people don't realize how many ashes are created when a person is cremated. Her parents could have a big urn of their daughter's ashes, but there would be plenty left over to fill a pretty green vase that Anita and I picked out."

I didn't want to remind her that Deb's body had been brought to the church funeral and taken to the church cemetery for interment. She had her dream about how Deb would end up. So did Anita.

For me, it was enough to realize that Deb had learned to move freely in the light and had transcended the physical world into the world of spirit successfully.

A week or so later, however, curiosity got the better of me. I found myself driving to the church cemetery in Forest Lake. It wasn't a big cemetery, but I remembered the name from the funeral program.

It was a remarkably sunny day in late winter when I parked my car and started walking up the rows of cemetery markers, looking for Deb's grave site.

Soon, however, I realized that locating her grave would not prove easy. The cemetery wasn't all that large, being a church cemetery. Yet walking up and down the rows of markers, reading them all on the right and on the left produced no results. Where was she?

It was extremely quiet there in the cemetery on that cold yet sunny winter afternoon. I could hear only birds in the distance. There were no other people there.

Out of the blue, I heard a voice. It was Deb. I heard her clearly inside my head.

"You will not find me here," she said.

I stopped in mid-stride. Ah, yes, I thought. That makes perfect sense. I turned around and returned to my car, knowing that Deb was in a far better place.

Chapter 15
Reflections

I never heard or saw Deb in any form after that sunny day at the cemetery. That trip provided a closure for me to let go of Deb. The mysterious music never filled the corners of her bedroom again, which was a good thing with a new tenant moving into that space.

I don't believe that Wizard ever saw or heard from Deb again, either. He never slipped into her old bedroom or played with the many toys that she had collected in his wicker basket. Wizard had his closure when he visited Deb for the last time at the hospice and then the day when she died and visited him with the pink ribbon.

Wizard moved onto other people, cats, and plants that needed his special healing touch. He would spend hours sitting next to anyone who was sick or just depressed. When he did that, his whole body would heat up, as though he was generating extra energy. He shared that energy also with kittens that he raised like a foster mother. Wizard was famous for raising babies, as though he was their birth mother. He also would sit with my aloe vera plants whenever they looked weak.

Deb was right about Wizard. He was a natural healer. And he knew that Deb had moved on, because he let her go.

I tried to do the same. Once the spirit of someone separates from the body in physical death, it's important to let them go. I realize that some people like to call out to the dearly departed or even try to communicate with them one last time; but it's best to let them go when they are ready.

Deb was a free spirit now, a light body that moved freely in the light. She could go anywhere she wanted without regard to time or space as we commonly think of them. She could evolve as a spiritual being, rising higher into the spiritual plane.

The mystics of early religions seemed to understand that. *The Sophia of Jesus Christ*, a book that dates back possibly as early as the first century, refers to the first light of creation and the radiance of angels without shadows. This book has probable roots in Gnostic, Essene, and Greek religious philosophy. It considers people to be light beings and views the divine source as pure light. Other examples of this message of light appear in *Pistis Sophia* which describes the divine light source and the kingdom of light and *The Epistle of Eugnostos,* two other early texts generally considered Gnostic.

This reverence for living in the light appear also in early Roman Mithraic Mysteries, early Christian iconography, post-Vedic texts, and the description of Pythagoras of the ray of creation and the seven rays that we recognize as reflected light forms of the creation ray. Both Eastern and

Western traditions seem to worship the light as the divine origin and the divine way of transcendence.

In India, the seven rays of light were associated with the seven Rishis or divine saints. Helena Blavatsky, author of *The Secret Doctrine*, considered the seven rays or Rishis to be primal forces in the universe that inhabit and empower all of life in ways that are both obvious and also are unseen.

Mystical powers described for advanced yogi practitioners in *The Yoga Sutras of Patanjali* focus on ways to develop human radiance. The yogi is directed to stimulate fire in the body to become radiant. This creates the halo effect around the body among the living. This is also described as a way to cast off the physical body through purification of fire and light.

It seems that a lot of people want to walk in the light, as best they understand that concept. These are generally people, I suppose, who have developed some understanding about transformation and spiritual evolution. But is that concept merely figurative, or is it literal? The experience of my friend Deb Bennett, a proven survivor, suggests that it is literally transcendent.

Some people claim to be able to see the light that is emitted by the human body and other living things. We commonly call these people psychic sensitives or aura readers. The Kirlian camera, based on researched by an amazing Russian couple who worked behind the old iron curtain, proved how energy that radiates from the human body and other living things can be measured on film for all to see.

Deb did not need a Kirlian camera or prayers to the Egyptian sun god Ra, the Rishis, or divine Sophia to personally experience the transcendent power of light. She experienced it personally in a way that seemed transformative to her. I would submit that – in addition to making her feel emotionally more comfortable about dying physically, the exercises actually showed her a way to negotiate the maze of dark uncertainty described in the ancient *Tibetan Book of the Dead.* Deb's exercises quite literally showed her how to gather her consciousness and energy body – apart from her physical body, to walk through light that she stimulated to radiate. She awakened a fire within her by absorbing, processing, and transforming the light that people naturally receive daily. She focused it with a keen sense of awareness.

Anyone could do that. It would be especially helpful for people who are facing death one day - and that includes all of us – to prepare ourselves to open new doors to new rooms and fill them with light to find our way. We will walk out of here, but not with our physical legs. We will walk out of here as light bodies, free of the dense encasement that has given us form in a material world.

Deb's exercises are easy enough to master. Anyone can learn to do them with a little practice. It's as easy as reclining on your back with legs and arms outstretched. You simply clear your mind of internal clutter and shut off the external distractions to allow you to really focus inwardly. You go deep inside yourself where spirit resides. You see a blank screen in your mind's eye and focus your attention on that alone. With your physical body asleep, your super-consciousness races. You become super aware and inwardly focused. You become consciously aware of the light that you have absorbed and processed inside you. The more you intently focus your attention on the light, the brighter it radiates.

You begin to experience the radiance and play with it creatively. You can make it brighter and even change the color from yellow to orange, red, blue, violet, and gold. The colored light resonates with your internal chakra system with seven colors of light that correspond to a rainbow of refracted light.

This is the ray of divine creation in its full spectrum of magnificence and possibilities. The colors correspond to the colors of your aura, as light is emitted from you. You are a light being that can naturally absorb, process, and transform light.

It's almost as though you can manifest light on command, but you are merely transforming the light that you are given. Is this magic? Magic is merely a creative and dynamic transformation of what was already there. This radiant energy is everywhere from the sun to the core of the earth, energizing every living thing including you. The divine spark in you, your essential life energy that is eternal, is simply a part of the radiance all around you.

As you intently focus your awareness on the light inside you and transform it, the radiance inside you grows. The light now shines inside you without leaking out. You have become a perfect light vessel. Light has reached its destination. There are no more shadows from light bouncing off you. You have consciously absorbed it, processed it, and now transform it into a glowing radiance.

The radiance is transcendent. You can now move in the light. You can travel anywhere at the speed of light, transcending physical limits of time and space. Your energy body moves freely in the light.

You can find your way, illuminated by the light. There are no physical barriers. Your spirit is free. It can move forward, roam, explore, and evolve.

Light meditations can be practiced and perfected. A yoga position is ideal. Deb's position in her hospice bed put her into a basic yoga posture known as "dead man's pose," where you lay flat on your back with your legs apart and hands apart. Ideally, your appendages would be at 45% angles. Ideally, you need to be in a quiet and secluded area to practice such deep, active meditations.

Luckily, the mysterious Indian yoga master who called me from beyond gave me a template. He taught me about meditating in the light and what the light could do for you in terms of total transformation.

Consequently, I recommend that people practice outdoors in the early morning sun beside running natural water if possible. Find a nice river or creek, if you can. Or you can meditate in the early morning sunlight beside the ocean. Even a lake or pond would be helpful.

These exercises can lead to conscious dying. They can guide you through the maze with the path clearly lighted.

They can also lead to living a life of greater awareness in preparation for the moment of separation when spirit leaves the mortal coil. *The Tibetan Book of the Dead* was not simply a guide to conscious dying and negotiating the mysterious *bardo* between the worlds but learning to live in the light. Becoming conscious of your light body frees you to explore and evolve anytime and anywhere. It puts you into harmonic resonance with divine energy and spirit to recognize the infinite possibilities in the present moment. Light strikes us to create the instant we know as the Now; and we learn to ride this wave of energy beyond time and space, at one with the infinite.

The Indian master tried to teach me that. And later I tried to teach it to my roommate Deb at her moment of need. Deb saw the light and learned how to focus it. For her, the experience was transcendent.

Bonus Chapter
Practical Exercises

EXERCISE: ABSORBING THE LIGHT

This is best done outdoors or near a window where natural light falls upon your face. Recline on your back, ideally in the yoga position commonly known as "dead man's pose," where your legs and arms are extended at 45-degree angles, with your body limp. Give your physical body permission to relax and release a little of its natural control. Learn to let go of the tension in your body and clear your mind of distractions and thoughts. Focus your intent only on the natural light around you and absorbing it through your eyes. Let your eyes almost close, with just the eyelashes slightly open to filter light streaming in. Drink in the light and focus your intent on holding this light inside you. Focus on building the intensity. You are a transformer, a dynamo of energy. Feel the light building within you, as you begin to realize your full potential as a being of light.

EXERCISE: TRANFORMING THE LIGHT

The light that you have absorbed and amplified within you at first appears simply as white light. All colors of light, however, combine to form white light. Within this light are the magical, transformative properties of all colors of light that correspond to the colors of the seven primal rays, the colors of the rainbow, and also the colors of your primary chakras. On each level of your subtle energy bodies is a non-physical chakra that radiates to one of the seven basic colors of the rays. Each chakra acts as a swirling vortex of energy on that level of your total being.

Read the light and then filter it with discernment. It's easier than you might at first believe. This involves the power of your will and creative visualization. Focus your mind's eye squarely on the light that you see inside of you, as though it were projected on a viewing screen. Stare at it and then slowly focus your attention on changing the color of the light. Your will center is located in your lower abdomen. Use your thought power and power of your will to transform the color of the light from white to yellow. At first, you might feel that you have failed, since yellow can appear very pale. But if you maintain your focus, you will eventually notice that the light has become a pale yellow. When you reach this point, then work in the same manner to make the yellow more intense. When it has grown very intense, it might appear to bounce with energy. Once you have reached this level, then slowly work in the same manner to transform the yellow light into orange light. Once the orange light grows in intensity to a darker, more vibrant orange, then transform it to green. Once you achieve a vibrant green, transform the light to blue. After blue, transform the light to indigo, then violet, and then red.

Feel each color run through your body energetically before you move on to the next color. These colors represent primal energy in the universe, and each color correspond to an area of the human body. Each chakra with its own distinctive pastel color from red to violet correspond to the subtle bodies and the planes of existence. Controlling all of the colors of light makes you a master of light who is able to move freely with your non-physical chakras and subtle energy bodies to the various planes of existence beyond our dense, mundane world of physical matter.

EXERCISE: PROJECTING THE LIGHT

You have successfully learned to absorb and transform light into various colors. Now you will learn to project the light that you have absorbed, amplified, and transformed. Most people "leak" light without focused intent, losing the impact of this primal force in nature. You, however, will learn to control the projection of this light purposefully. Like the above exercises in light, this is not extremely difficult, but requires much practice and focused intent. You can send your thought forms as thought power. You can also send light in the same way through your consciousness. Now energy healers, empathic healers, and others engaged in the healing arts might see in this the immediate benefit of being able to direct energy to another person. Projecting light also enables us to heal ourselves, if we move outside our physical body in our subtle bodies. Projecting light also brightens the path in front of us, as we move outside our physical world. This could be especially helpful to the dying, as they prepare to leave their physical body. In this way, they move into the light and transcend this physical plane to other subtle worlds.

EXERCISE: OPENING NEW DOORS

To successfully leave the physical body behind and find yourself on the other side, so to speak, you need to learn to open doors. These are not wooden or metal doors of a physical construction, of course, but doorways that lead to other planes of existence. These are doorways that lead from the physical world to the world of spirit. The spirit world is a realm of unmanifest energy, filled with potential, as opposed to the manifest realm of matter in our physical world. It is a world of light. It is a world beyond time and space and other restrictions of the physical world.

Everyone is going to eventually die a physical death, so everyone should learn to open the doorway that successfully leads outside this physical world into the greater world of spirit on the other side. In my exercises with Deb, based largely on The Tibetan Book of the Dead and exercises suggested in The Yoga Sutras, I showed a way to learn how to open doorways and leave the physical world behind. You can practice this now, so that you will be ready. As a healthy, living person, you will be able to practice leaving, with the assurance that you can now successfully return to your physical body.

Once again, this exercise requires the use of creative visualization. Close your eyes and visualize a doorway in front of you. In your mind's eye, reach out and open the door and pass through the doorway. Once you have passed through the doorway, look around and see that you are safe and surrounded by the light that you have brought to light the way. Each new room that you enter symbolically might appear to have a slightly different color on its own. Or you can fill the room with light that you bring once you enter it, should the new room appear dark to you at first. The principle to realize here is that there is always light, if you can find it. We are never truly faced with darkness. This is a very basic occult truth about the nature of cosmology.

Notice the color in each new room and intensify it before moving on to the next doorway. In each room, realize that you are safe and filled with light.

EXERCISE: MOVING BEYOND TIME AND SPACE

Beyond the physical world, there is no sense of time or space. It might seem that you are moving slowly but moving with light at the speed of light allows you to exceed the limitations of time. And moving outside the physical world means that you are no longer faced by the three-dimensional limitations of space-time, as we normally experience life. You are free as the light. You are no longer restricted. As you move in the light, opening doorways beyond the physical world, notice that you no longer have a sense of up or down or right or left. Notice that you have no sense of depth. Notice that you are no longer conscious of time passing. You are entering the Eternal Now.

Bibliography

Aurobindo, Sri, *The Secret of the Veda.* Pondicherry, India; Sri Aurobindo Ashram Publication, 1971.

Besant, Annie. *Thought Power.* Wheaton, Ill.: Quest Books, 1967.

Besant, Annie, and Charles W. Leadbeater. *Thought Forms.* Adyar, India: Theosophical Publishing House. 1901.

Blavatsky, Helena Petrovna. *The Secret Doctrine.* Adyar, India: Theosophical Publishing House, 1979.

Braschler, Von. *Confessions of a Reluctant Ghost Hunter.* Rochester, Vt.: Destiny Books, 2014.

---------*Seven Secrets of Time Travel.* Rochester, Vt.: Destiny Books, 2012.

Bryant, Edwin F. *The Yoga Sutras of Patanjali.* New York, NY: North Point Press, 2009.

Coomaraswamy, Ananda K. *The Door in the Sky,* from originals in the Bollinger Series. Princeton, NJ: Princeton University Press, 1940-1947 ed.

Einstein, Albert, *The Theory of Relativity & Other Essays.* New York, NY: MJF Books, 1950.

Guthrie, Kenneth Sylvan. *The Pythagorean Sourcebook and Library.* Grand Rapids, Mich.: Phanes Press, 1987.

Grosz, Anton. *Letters to a Dying Friend: Helping Those You Love Make a Conscious Transition.* Wheaton, Ill.: Quest Books, 1989.

Karagulla, Shafica, and Dora Van Gelder Kunz. *The Chakras and the Human Energy Fields.* Wheaton, Ill.: Theosophical Publishing House, 1998.

Kubler-Ross, Elizabeth. *On Death and Dying.* New York, NY: Simon & Schuster, 1970Lumpkins, Joseph B. *The Sophia of Jesus Christ and Eugnostos the Blessed.* Blounstville, AL: Fifth Estate, Inc., 2014

Leadbeater, C.W. *The Chakras.* Wheaton, Ill.: Theosophical Publishing House, 1997.

Mead, G.R.S. *Pistis Sophia.: A Gnostic Miscellany Being for the Most Part Extracts from the Books of the Savior.* London, UK: John M.Watkins, 1921.

Meyer, Marvin. *The Nag Hammadi Scriptures.* New York, NY: HarperCollins, 2007.

Nagy, Andras M. *The Secrets of Pythagoras.* Charleston, N.C.: CreateSpace, 2007.

Ouspensky, P.D. *In Search of the Miraculous.* New York, NY: Harcourt, Brace & World, Inc., 1949.

-------- *The Psychology of Man's Possible Evolution.* New York, NY: Vintage Books, 1974.

--------- *Tertium Organum.* Kila, Mont.: Kessinger Publishing Company, 1998.

Richards, Steve. *Invisibility.* London, UK: Thorsons, 1992.

Rinpoche, Sogyal and Patrick Gaffney. *The Tibetan Book of Living and Dying.* San Francisco, Calif.: Harper, 2012.

Paulson, Genevive Lewis. *Energy Focused Meditation.* St. Paul, Minn.: Llewellyn Publications, 2000.

Shroder, Tom. *Old Souls: Compelling Evidence from Children Who Remember Past Lives.* New York, NY: Simon & Schuster, 2001.

Stevenson, Ian. *Children Who Remember Previous Lives.* Jefferson, NC: McFarland, 2001.

Tiller, William A., Walter Dibble, and Michael Kohane. *Conscious Acts of Creation.* Walnut Creek, Calif.: Pavior Publishing, 2001.

Twitchell, Paul. *The Tiger's Fang.* Menlo Park, Calif.: Illuminated Way Press, 1967.

Woods, Ernest. *The Seven Rays.* Wheaton, Ill.: Quest Books, 1976.